WALKING *in* *my* SHOES

A Woman's Story of Leadership

LAURA DOWNEY HILL

Walking in My Shoes
A Woman's Story of Leadership

©2022 Laura Downey Hill

print ISBN: 978-1-66785-841-8
ebook ISBN: 978-1-66785-842-5

Contents

INTRODUCTION

Walking in my Shoes is a story about leadership and what I experienced as a woman over six decades. I think you will find it full of memorable stories and hard learned lessons. I share with honesty, humility, and a bit of humor the path I took and the choices I made along the way. We each have a story, one that, regardless of age, has shaped who we are today. We are a reflection of so many things: family, friends, colleagues, experiences, and decisions made along the way. We desperately need more women leaders. Be inspired to look back on your own path so far and challenge yourself to make bold changes for your future.

WHERE I BEGAN

I am sitting in my parents' kitchen listening to them reminisce about old memories from the 1950s — the war, when they met, when they left New York City and when they had me. The years and the decisions that would change our family, decisions made by two city kids who just wanted a better life. We are enjoying a salad straight out of my dad's garden, spicy mustard lettuce, endive, radishes, assorted peppers, tiny onions, and juicy tomatoes. Outside the window Longhorns meander by, grazing on the lush green grass as they lumber slowly and methodically down to the pond to cool off on this hot Texas day. A wind turbine hums. Two completely different worlds colliding. We are sorting through how these two city kids got here, today, almost 70 years after they took a chance. My dad is 91 now, my mom is 88. They are enjoying bouncing stories back and forth, filling in the gaps for each other; I am jumping in with questions. Occasionally a memory becomes emotional; I can see them pause as they drift back in time. My mom is amazing at recalling details; guess it is a mom thing. They remember the 1950s as a hopeful time, a time of change; the booming interstate highway project connected cities and allowed people like my parents to leave the city neighborhoods where they grew up, and where generations of our family lived. My parents were the first to leave; they were the only ones who would. It was a time of building highways, tunnels, and bridges. Our country was growing up and my parents were on the verge of changing the direction and opportunities for our family for generations to come.

It is strange taking this trip back in time, back to and through memories. The past is so important to knowing why we are who we are, where we came from, what we learned growing up and from whom. Stepping back through the years and experiences, each one helps define how I became the woman I am. Back to the beginning, my beginning — 1957, the peak year for the baby boomer generation. WWII Army General Dwight D. Eisenhower was President, Richard Nixon was Vice President. It was the year the Soviet Union launched Sputnik, the first man-made object to be placed into earth's orbit. The United States would respond the next year creating the National Aeronautics and Space Administration, NASA. The space race had begun. The Civil Rights Act of 1957 was signed. It was the first federal civil rights legislation passed in Congress since 1875 protecting voter rights and establishing the civil rights division of the Justice Department. It seems surreal to me that two young kids from Baldwin, New York, who had never left home except to fight in a war, with just the money in their pockets, a used car and the promise of a college education could become part of the American Dream.

My dad graduated from high school in June of 1950; in July he enlisted in the Army. North Korea had just invaded South Korea. The Army sent him to basic training, jump school and then assigned him to the 187th Airborne Infantry Regiment. When the war ended in July, 1953, Dad's division stayed to secure equipment and the border. In

April 1954 he was shipped home with a purple heart and the G.I. Bill. He returned changed but determined to turn the stress of war into an opportunity otherwise out of reach for him — a college education. He had a few months before he would head to college, but as fate would have it, that summer he met my mom. It was a casual neighborhood meeting. Dad's best friend was dating Mom's best friend. He and my mom were engaged three months after they met, and Dad went off to his freshman year at the University of Maryland. They married the next summer. She was 20 he was 23.

Rent was $40.00 a month for their first home (soon to be mine), an old army barracks on the campus of the University of Maryland which had been turned into apartments for students on the G.I. Bill. He was the first in his family to go to college; I would be the second. My dad was President of the Sigma Chi fraternity at the University of Maryland his senior year. From freshman year he was always involved in fraternity leadership and even worked odd jobs around the fraternity house to make extra money. He got lucky and landed a job as an assistant student trainer for the college's basketball team, the Terrapins. The job paid pretty well and afforded him a great deal of time to study while the athletes were in the whirlpools. He also had great seats for every game.

My mom worked fulltime for the Baltimore and Ohio Railroad. Evenings were spent helping my dad write papers and study for exams. Mom remembers being 22, pregnant with me and voting for the first time in the 1956 Presidential election. General Dwight D. Eisenhower was running for a second term. I would be born the next April at the end of my dad's junior year. My mom always planned on returning to the railroad after I was born; money was tight, and the railroad paid very well. But when the time came to return, she could not do it. She wanted to be a fulltime mom. When my dad graduated from college in 1958, jobs were tough to find. My mom recalls packing up the apartment and the old Ford Falcon station wagon, ready to head back to New York when my dad got a call to interview with Reuben H. Donnelley Corporation. That interview began a 30-year career in the Yellow Pages.

Graduation 1958, University of Maryland

The sales job with Donnelley meant they did not have to go back to New York, to family. They had made it out and could continue their own path. Dad was meant to be in sales. Brought up in a family with a father who walked out when he was only 11, my dad jokes that his first sales job was going to the landlord's house and explaining why the rent was late, again. The new job afforded a bigger apartment in College Park, $80.00 a month, where we would live for the next two years and where we welcomed (everyone except me) my new sister in

1960. I can remember like it was yesterday, April 19, 1960, the day they told me I had a new sister. When they brought her home from the hospital, I positioned myself in her crib, gripping the wooden slats, screaming to take her back. Mom said I insisted on a brother so having a sister was bad enough, but she had the nerve to be born six days before my birthday. There was no way I was not going to be a brat every year at my sister's birthday parties. My mom said I was such a nightmare that she had to come up with a plan. Consequentially, my whole childhood, to keep the peace, I shared a birthday party with my sister.

Celebrating Birthdays 'Together'

In 1962, with two kids, the old Falcon still running strong, and a loan from my dad's grandmother, my parents moved us to our first house in the DC suburb of New Carrollton, Maryland. New Carrollton was one of the first suburbs, and young families flocked there for affordable starter homes. The beltway had just been built around DC which made commuting to the city possible. There were three different, cookie-cutter styles of houses, repeated down the sidewalk lined streets. Ours was a tiny split level, walk out basement, no garage. The nice houses had carports (at least as I saw it). How fancy to have a covered place to park your car! My sister and I shared a room and soon we had a baby brother, born in 1964. Mom and Dad could finally afford a second car; a used 1957 Chevrolet Bel Air. It was fun to live in a big neighborhood; there were so many kids, and every parent had the same rule; stay outside until it starts to get dark. I remember hours and hours of cops and robbers on bikes and playing kickball in the street until we could not see the ball anymore. The Smith's dinner bell signaled time for dinner in every house on the street. I have memories of riding my bike up to the grocery store parking lot every Saturday to go to the book mobile. The smell of fish sticks cooking in the oven told me my parents were going out to play bridge. Most nights we had pot roast or meatloaf. Swanson's TV dinners served on folding metal TV trays were a big treat because you were guaranteed dessert.

Our first house New Carrollton, Maryland

Reuben H. Donnelley had an office in downtown Washington DC on Wisconsin Avenue. They shared a building with a local TV station, WTTG-TV Channel 5. Donnelley 'kids' were in the perfect spot to get invitations to the taping of the Bozo the Clown and Cousin Cupcake Show. Willard Scott Jr. was Bozo; he later went on to be Ronald MacDonald for the DC MacDonald's franchise, and of course, later weatherman on The Today Show for 30 years. This TV station was the site of my first public speaking engagement that lives in infamy in my family. I was invited to be on the Romper Room Show with Miss Connie — do be a do bee, don't be a don't bee – and everyone was excited. I was on the TV show for a week. We said the Pledge of Allegiance at the start of each show and prayed before our snack. We watched in excitement as Miss Connie held the Magic Mirror and told the kids watching from home that she could see them. During one show Miss Connie asked the preschoolers, "What's new at your house today?" I announced that we were getting a new fence for our back yard because my mom and dad were mad that our neighbors kept cutting through our yard and waving in our windows. My parents were mortified; they still cringe today retelling the story. Of course, the whole neighborhood was watching.

My TV debut, Romper Room with Miss Connie

A new fence meant a new dog and so began my incredible love of dogs. My mom was listening to her morning radio show when they announced that there was a collie who was ready for adoption; she called in right away. Shannon was a tricolored collie. I loved him so much and I do not remember any of my childhood without him. He was always part of our dress up fun and he would let me put curlers in his hair. I pretended I was a waitress bringing him his dinner on a tray every night, holding it up high, watching him dance around so happily. I cried when I left him to go to college. Shannon lived until I was a sophomore in college. I still remember the girls yelling down the hall of Smith dorm that I had a phone call. It was my mom. She told me Shannon had died. Losing your first pet is something you never forget and not being there with him at the end made it so much worse.

Our childhood dog, Shannon

I was always a challenge. My mom now refers to me as a precocious child. Ahh, the years have dulled her memory, and my dad just shakes his head and says I have not changed. I remember always being in trouble, most of the time for talking too much. My little wooden desk memorized the path to the corner of the classroom. My first two years of elementary school were at Saint Mary's Catholic School, but it did not last. I will never forget the day Sister Mary Thomas Moore left the classroom. I am sure she threatened silence but as soon as she was gone, I jumped up to the front of the room and grabbed her long wooden pointer stick with the little red rubber tip and proceeded to call the class to attention by hitting the blackboard with her stick. To my horror the little rubber end of the stick went flying. I still remember crawling on my hands and knees in a panic searching under desks for the tip before she returned. I got caught and was forced to stay inside searching while the class went to recess. Finally, when my classmates came back in from recess, someone spotted the tip which had flown out the classroom door.

Saint Mary's was right across the street from the Giant Food Store, the supermarket where my mom did her grocery shopping. My mom remembers driving to the Giant one day while my sister and I were at school. As she turned into the parking lot, she saw a child standing all alone outside the school; she did a double take. It was me all alone, no one else in sight, standing near the busy parkway (that could never happen today). She quickly did a U-turn in the parking lot and crossed over to the school to see what was going on. It seems I was talking too much so my teacher just put me outside so I could not bother my classmates. That was the second grade. Third grade I was transferred to Margaret Brent Elementary School. The end of my Catholic school education was unceremonious.

Those early years living in the DC suburbs meant amazing field trips during elementary school and Saturdays with family, spent at the Smithsonian, the National Museum of Natural History, touring our nation's memorials, visiting the White House, which was open to the public, and seeing the amazing National Cherry Blossom Festival around the tidal basin. My dad loves history, and we visited every battlefield on the east coast when I was a kid. To this day I remember our red, scotch-plaid cooler filled with sandwiches and apples for our excursions. He made sure we knew the history of every place we visited. My parents taught us respect for our country. I remember my mom dressing my sister and me in our Sunday best and taking us to see Mrs. Kennedy at the Washington Episcopal Church flower show. We lined the street with hundreds of others, waving at her as her car left the event. I remember visiting President John F. Kennedy's grave at the Arlington National Cemetery. I recall it was dark and dreary, the winter wind chilled us to the bone. The only sound was crying punctuated by loud sobs. I was young but I can still remember the snow covering the ground everywhere except a ring around the eternal flame. The sadness was profound. We were dressed in our Sunday best; my parents said it was a sign of respect. I have early memories of standing in line for hours to enter the capitol rotunda where former President Herbert Hoover was lying in state (1964). I was too young to truly understand but I sensed the importance and watched as my parents stopped in front of the casket, making the sign of the cross. Nine years and three transfers later, we would pay our respects at the rotunda again, this time to former President Lyndon B. Johnson lying in state.

I grew up watching my dad work. That is really the thing I remember most about him. He was a door-to-door yellow pages salesman for years before being promoted to management. He left the house every day in a suit and tie, carrying a briefcase and always wearing a hat. When I was young, maybe five or six, my dad would take me to the office in DC every Saturday morning while he did his sales report for the week. I remember the sound of calculators and big white boards full of numbers. When your dad works on commission, you become aware at a very young age the impact of a good week and can sense the stress of a bad week. Pay day was Friday and Saturday was grocery shopping day. If Dad had a good week, Mom bought ice cream — Neapolitan. I still do not know why, maybe to get both chocolate and vanilla. I remember fighting with my brother and sister over the bowl with less strawberry. No one liked the strawberry. On Saturday night we would sit on the floor in front of our TV set, which was set in a huge maple cabinet with big rabbit ears and watch Bonanza. Saturday morning was the only time the kids got the TV, evenings it was Walter Cronkite on the CBS Evening News first, then whatever my dad wanted to watch. It was our job to get up and change the channel for him and rearrange the rabbit ears until the picture was clear. I remember in 1966 when Captain James T. Kirk, Spock and Dr. Bones McCoy travelled the Milky Way in the USS Enterprise, boldly going where no man has gone before. My dad loved that show and while I never became a trekkie, the show reminds me of good times spent with my dad. I admit I had bad dreams about Miri, Jahn and the "onlies" (the only ones left) for years.

 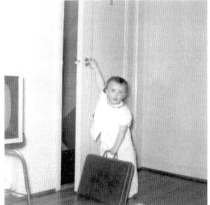

Helping my Dad get to work

I knew from a very young age that my dad was driven; he carried the weight of making it on his shoulders. I did not really understand it as a young child but now I understand it, breaking away from your past is easier said than done. In 1967 my dad was promoted from sales to management and that introduced me to the worst word in my childhood — transfer. I hated moving, even the thought of it makes me ill today. It meant losing friends, feeling awkward, starting over and over and over. That year we made our first move to Suffield, Connecticut. I would be a 5th grader at McAlister Middle School. We only lived in Suffield for a year, but I have great memories of my dad hooking up the hose in the dead of winter and spraying the snow behind our back porch so it would freeze overnight. The next day we could ice skate all day on our private ice-skating rink. Shannon would run around the edge barking for us to stop. Suffield would be where we got rid of the Bel Air and Dad got his first company car. The old Ford Falcon was gone too and for the first time we had two new cars. It is where I learned a valuable, lifelong lesson during my first week in my new school, a mistake I never made again. Do not pass notes in class to the cute boy; he probably has a 'girlfriend' and that will set you back by at least a month from being welcomed to your new school. Ahh, the beginning of strategic thinking.

Suffield is where my love of shoes began, but not for the right reasons. The beginning of every new school year meant back-to-school shopping. In my family that was one new outfit for the first day of school. That particular year I needed new shoes. My mom pulled them from the sales rack, and I knew immediately I hated them. Muddy brown oxfords with an elongated square toe. She was thrilled, they had room in them to grow. Great, ugly, and too big. The sale must have been a good one because she decided to get me a pair of new church shoes as well. Black patent leather, cute strap, and nice rounded toe. I loved them but they were for Sunday only. I went off to my first day at McAlister Middle School scared, nervous, and hating my shoes. It only took me a few days to decide something had to be done about the shoes; I figured out I could hide my Sunday shoes under my coat until I got on the bus. I would put my ugly oxfords in my locker and change on the bus on my way home. I cannot remember getting caught by my mom although I am sure I did, but what sticks with me is how great those Sunday shoes made me feel; they were confidence lifting. Shoes still make me feel that way today.

With each promotion came a new city, new house, new school and saying goodbye to friends. After Connecticut came a transfer to Charleston, West Virginia, then Silver Springs, Maryland, and finally Camp Hill, Pennsylvania. Two elementary schools, two middle schools, two high schools. I cried often and slammed many doors. Why couldn't we stay in one place? Dad was not ever home anyway and the more we moved, the more he travelled. My mom was always packing and unpacking. Getting us enrolled in our new school, then pulling us out, repeat — repeat — repeat. I do not know how she did it, times were different, marriages were not equal partnerships. I think she just accepted it; I do not know that she had any other option. I hated meeting new kids in each new town and never having the chance to develop close friendships — friendships that last a lifetime. To this day I am sad that I do not have childhood friends — just the memories of the moving truck coming and going.

In West Virginia, we bought a house in a neighborhood called Sherwood Forest and lived on Robin Hood Road. How can you ever forget that? My dad's job included a country club membership. Until then I do not think I knew country clubs existed. Driving up the long winding entrance to Berry Hills Country Club was magical. Mom would drop us off in the morning for golf camp and not pick us up until dinner time. I had never tried a sport before that first summer. My dad was always a weekend public course golfer when he could find the time, but golf became part of doing business as he climbed the corporate ladder. For me it was heaven, day after day surrounded by friends. We played golf, hit the snack bar for a hotdog (included in camp) and swam for hours until our parents picked us up. Making so many friends during that first summer made the first day of school at John Adams Middle School one of the best I remember. Unfortunately, after two and a half years we were packing again, crying goodbye to friends, promising to write letters. I hated it.

In 1971 we moved to Silver Springs, Maryland. I was a freshman in high school. It was the first house where my sister and I had our own bedrooms. I could sense things were getting easier for my family financially but there was still an underlying sadness that comes from the constant upheaval and lack of roots. Memories revolved around holidays, visits from grandparents, and family trips to more battlefields. This move was one of the worst. We moved right before school started and moved again as soon as the school year ended. I cannot remember much about my freshman year or John F. Kennedy High School except the football fight song and being embarrassed when another girl I was trying to befriend asked me why I did not shave my legs. One thing about moving often was I missed a lot of peer pressure issues, but I also missed what was in and what was not. I went home that day demanding to start shaving.

Finally, the summer before my sophomore year in high school, we moved to Camp Hill, Pennsylvania, where I would get to stay a few years and graduate with the Cumberland Valley High School class of 1975. I was always a good student but very talkative and definitely a bit overbearing. Looking back, I realize I just desperately wanted to be accepted. I dreamed of being a normal teenager with a couple of close girlfriends, to have sleepovers and stay up late telling secrets. I only understood short term friendships which were not really friendships at all. Cumberland Valley was a huge high school in a very blue-collar community, Mechanicsburg, Pennsylvania. There were school clubs for every interest, sport, and campus activity. I was a kid in a candy store and skipped from one thing to another — French club, choir, the school newspaper, gymnastics, track, and competitive extemporaneous speaking. I never committed to any one thing but knew I had the time to try it all. It was a time of sampling and deciding who I wanted to be. More importantly, I could see the end of the constant moving.

We had only lived in our new house for a week, and I was still sulking and making everyone's life miserable. Moving boxes were everywhere in different stages of being unpacked. I was in the family room laying on the sofa watching TV. My dad had just gotten home from work, so I knew it was time to jump up and set the kitchen table for dinner. Before I could get up, my dad walked into the room, looked at me on the sofa and said, "I hope you don't think you are going to lay around all summer. You're 16, go get a job." In my house, when Dad said get a job, you got a job. I answered an ad in the local newspaper; the Ramada Inn was looking for waitresses. My mom drove me to my first interview; she dropped me off at the hotel entrance. I walked in scared to death and walked out with my first job, and so began my 'career' in the hospitality industry. In the 70s we were waiters and waitresses, not servers. Tips went right into your pocket; they were not tracked or taxed. I went home 'high school' rich after every shift. By the time summer was over, I had been awarded a coveted spot on the dinner shift with the seasoned waiters and waitresses. I had earned it with hard work, picking up extra shifts and sticking around to do extra 'side-work,' all the cleanup and prep that happens before and after restaurant hours. My boss acted like the promotion was a gift; he wanted to be sure I owed him in case he needed me for an extra shift. Ramada legend said that tips were double on the dinner shift; they were! I had never had so much money before; in those days babysitting paid around 50 cents an hour. My parents were hawk eyes when it came to me having cash in my pocket after every shift. Much to my disappointment I got my first lesson in saving money. Every dollar went right to the bank, into a savings account for college. I got to keep the change for spending money.

My mom and dad were still picking me up and dropping me off at work. We only had two cars and my dad usually got home late. I did not grow up in a house where a car for a kid would ever be a consideration. Even when I got my license, my parents rarely let me use a car. Of course, I probably cannot blame them. They let my sister and me use the car one Friday night for a football game. By the time I got home the big old green Mercury Monterey was billowing smoke; the smell was awful. My dad ran over with the hose. I was so upset, telling my parents that the car would not go unless I stepped hard on the gas. Yes, I had driven all the way home (16 miles) on the Carlisle Pike with the emergency brake on. Another good life lesson.

I had worked at the Ramada Inn for just over a year when a new owner came in and completely remodeled the restaurant. The staff was called in on a Saturday for a day of training and to be issued new uniforms. We walked into a completely new concept, the name, Wicked Wanda's Warehouse. Oh yes. Welcome to the 70s. But what really raised my parents' eyebrows was the new uniform — a form fitting pale pink polyester halter gown!! Each waitress was paired with a waiter. The management trainer said we would operate like a couple, the women in gowns and the men in modified tuxedos. The men were the only ones who could carry the tray of food (I guess because they were stronger?); the women would serve. How ridiculous! Wicked Wanda's Warehouse opened to much fanfare. I did not fare so well. Working in a gown was weird, and I could see they were bringing in much more attractive waitresses and many of the older ladies were being pushed out. I hated to give up the tips, but I opted for a safer position, working the candy counter at Bowman's Department Store. I left my first job over a racy uniform. It was a Ramada Inn on the Carlisle Pike not the Las Vegas strip. Management never asked us how we felt in the uniforms. I learned a good lesson. I value feeling good and confident in what I wear; I want my employees to feel the same.

College could not come fast enough. I would get to choose where I wanted to go to college, where I could invest in myself for four years without any fear of transferring. It was empowering. As graduation neared, I would be one of only a handful of graduates in a class of 600 who would leave the state. My experience had been different, there was no reason to stay close to home because home was not a guarantee. Sure enough, by my sophomore year in college my parents were packing again, across the same state this time but still a far trip from the friends I had finally made in high school. The job that had given me, my sister and brother the opportunity to go to college had not always been kind to us growing up. But maybe the disappointments and constant upheaval made me stronger than most girls my age. As I entered college in 1975, I was confident in myself and ready to take on the challenges ahead.

LESSONS THAT LAST A LIFETIME

Dad reflects on their last transfer in 1983; Mom fills in the details. They could not have imagined that Texas would be where my dad's corporate career would end, and the ultimate gamble would begin. He reminisces about the lessons he learned as a young man — good examples are meant to be copied and the bad ones learned from, so you do not make the same mistakes again. Dad states it as fact that, growing up, the best advice he ever got was from his grandfather, a first generation American with an eighth-grade education.

My dad did not have role models in his mother and father. His father was an only child, spoiled and irresponsible when it came to handling money. My dad, the oldest, watched how his mom and dad were happy living with constant handouts from their parents. Dad remembers going into the neighborhood grocery store and begging them to put a few things on his parents' tab, even though their bill was way overdue. For most of his childhood his father did not live with the family. They would see him for holidays, family events, and summers in Southampton, New York, but there was always an undercurrent of stress whenever they were all together. His mother was Catholic, his father Presbyterian, and she used religion to refuse to grant him a divorce, so he just left. He never got remarried and did help with financial support, but he was fine letting both sets of parents provide for his wife and three kids. My dad watched the money struggles and saw how his grandparents stepped in to help with rent, food, and school clothes. As he got older, his grandparents took the time to teach him about managing money. They taught him to respect his financial obligations and to always be a saver, no matter how small the amount. To this day he pays his bills the day he receives them. Spending money comes with responsibility — a lesson my dad in turn taught me. He believes each generation must strive to do better than the last. Not every relative sets a good example, not even parents. You must pick the family members who you can model. Copy the best and learn from the worst.

Dad's Grandfather, Grandmother and his Father

Dad's Mother

Dad grew up in Saint Albans in the Queens Borough of New York City with his extended family. He was the oldest with a younger brother and sister. His family spent every summer in Southampton, New York. His grandfather (his dad's father) had bought a few acres on the Peconic Bay in the 1920s when land in the Hamptons was dirt cheap and the Hamptons were not the affluent destination they are today. Over the years friends pitched in and helped build a small cabin, trading out labor for meals and time fishing. Eventually my great-grandfather built a small house, no air conditioning or heat. My dad spent every summer with his grandparents in this simple but idyllic place. He learned how to build and repair things from his grandfather and after the work was done, they spent hours fishing and sailing, things the city could never teach him. My dad's fondest childhood memories were those simple summers in Southampton. He talks about the wisdom they passed on to him that has guided him as if it was yesterday. His grandmother was devoted to his grandfather. They both saw the world in such simple truths — always do the right thing, be a person of your word and work hard for everything.

My oldest son recently interviewed my dad so we would have a recording of him reminiscing about his life. Dad chuckles on the tape as he shares a story about his grandmother who he refers to as one tough cookie. For years she volunteered as an ambulance driver for the Red Cross in New York City. Even into her 70s she drove soldiers who had been shipped home from one hospital in New York to another. When my dad was in Korea, the family received a telegram telling them my father had been wounded and was trapped on an outpost under enemy fire. My dad and a fellow soldier were hit by shrapnel while dragging an unconscious soldier to safety. They were able to save his life. The Army transported my dad from the outpost back behind the main line of resistance to a big bunker where medics stitched him up. A couple of days had gone by, and my dad was well on his way to recovery when a man in a jeep pulled up dressed in civilian clothes. He got everyone's attention because they never saw anyone in civilian clothes. A buzz went through the bunker. Turns out the guy was with the Red Cross; Dad's grandmother had tracked down the right people at the Red Cross in Korea and demanded they send someone out to make sure her grandson was going to be okay. Of course, he was fine but the guys in his platoon got the biggest laugh at his expense. They thought it was hilarious that his grandma was checking on him. He never heard the end of that one, but that was his grandmother; when she wanted something, there was no stopping her. She was a huge influence on my father and very vocal, making sure he knew right from wrong. Her personality was larger than life, even as a young child I remember her energy and laughter. She was never shy with her opinions and my great-grandfather always sought her advice. My dad remembers my great grandparents as a team that always stuck together. He paid them the highest compliment, by taking their advice, getting out of New York, and going to college.

Great-grandpa snoozing, Great-grandma with me,
their first Great-grandchild

My dad graduated from high school as the Korean War broke out. Like many young men of that era, he wanted to put his mark on the world. Motivated by patriotism and the desire to do great things, he enlisted in the Army as a paratrooper. He did basic training at Ft. Dix, New Jersey, for four months, and then rode a train to Columbus, Georgia, Ft. Benning, for three weeks of paratrooper training. Dad said it was stressful and not everyone would make it through all three weeks. He shakes his head and chuckles remembering the old saying they had, "Jumping off the tower separates the boys from the men but jumping out of the plane separates the men from the crazies." He qualified with five jumps. For six months Dad's unit practiced jumping in the states before they shipped out. His unit was near the front lines and made many practice jumps in Korea and Japan where they went for the winter. He made a total of 18 jumps during his service but none in combat. Dad never complained about the hardships but just said they did what they had to do, and the Army treated him fairly. He did get into many fire fights, killed enemy soldiers and accepted it as an unavoidable part of war. All soldiers who serve in combat have many interesting stories and here are two from him.

Dad, 187th Airborne

Jump School, Fort Benning

Dad's Platoon, Korea

One day Dad went on patrol with his unit near the front lines where a small recon aircraft came late in the afternoon each day to assess the current status of the enemy. Someone got a wild idea to use this to trap the enemy. A dummy with a parachute was put in the other seat in the patrol aircraft and a smoke device was installed. The plan was when the airplane was shot at, as it always was, it would set off the smoke device and push the dummy out to parachute to the ground. The aircraft would then fly behind a hill where oil drums would be lit to simulate an aircraft crash. This scenario was intended to draw the enemy to look for the parachute and the crashed aircraft and thus be exposed and killed. This worked so well that Dad was confronted with three Chinese soldiers which he shot with his BAR automatic rifle. The area was then covered in smoke so the US troops could escape. The Generals watched this whole scenario, and it got great notoriety for its success!

Three days before the end of the war, Dad, as a reconnaissance scout, was sent out with a lieutenant and three other enlisted men to a key observation position behind enemy lines. They were to stay there and report at a given time. When they called in at the designated time, it was the General on the line telling them that they had two choices — one, to surrender, or two, to walk through a mine field to rejoin US troops. The General did offer to clear the mine field with an artillery barrage and have US troops meet them halfway! This is what they did, and they got back safely thinking "Who wants to be the last man killed in the war?"

When my dad came home from Korea, he had a plan. With a pained look on his face, he says that the war ended up being one of the best things that ever happened to him. Without the G.I. Bill which paid for college tuition, college would have been impossible. He planned to follow several soldiers from his platoon to college at the University of Maryland as soon as the summer was over. They helped him to secure a place to live and a campus job. That was the summer of 1954, the summer he met my mom and as luck and love would have it, she had no reason to stay in New York either.

My mom grew up much differently than my dad. She was an only child. Her family lived in apartments until my mother was in high school. Her mother was a stern woman, and her dad was the opposite, but her mom made the rules. Her dad worked for most of his life as a brick mason with the bricklayers' union in New York City. It was back breaking work, and eventually he worked his way up to project supervisor. Grand-daddy was a simple, hardworking man with a sixth-grade education. My grandmother made sure dinner was on the table every night when he got home. I remember my grand-daddy sitting at the square pine table in the corner of the kitchen, a table my mom still has, the chairs so tiny I cannot imagine how my 6'4" grand-daddy could sit in them comfortably. He raised pigeons on the roof of the apartment building and loved dogs.

My Mom's Mother and Father with me, their first Grandchild

One night he came home with a dog, a boxer, for my mom. She was 14 and had always begged for a dog. He told my irritated grandmother that the dog had just followed him home. She begrudgingly let the dog stay. Brandy, the boxer, was my mom's dog, the dog she had wanted for so long. Two years later, while my mom was out of town at a high school oratorical competition, my grandmother gave Brandy away. I have heard that story my whole life, even today it makes me feel horrible and my mom is still pained by it. We got our love of animals from her dad, my granddaddy. He was larger than life to me. I remember when he came to visit; the first thing he would do was take our collie, Shannon, on a long walk. He was always so excited to see Shannon and walked him several times a day, every day; I loved going along. He would have had a house full of animals if my grandmother would have let him. He would be so proud of me, my mom, and my children if he could see us today. We are all crazy about animals.

My mom commuted to Catholic school on buses and trains; she often stayed in Bayside, New York, with her grandmother to cut down on the long commute. Mom spent much time with her grandmother, a petite woman who loved to sew and fatten up everyone who came to visit. She was our Nana. I remember eating fresh strawberries with cream at her tiny dining room table. Sometimes she would toast a slice of homemade pound cake. We are not a family of great cooks; I do not qualify as even a mediocre cook, but my Nana always made something special for us. I loved to watch her sew; I can remember watching her make an apron, the material was pale pink covered in spring flowers. So strange that I remember that. I was mesmerized by the needle moving up and down so quickly and the rocking spool of thread on the 1920s Singer sewing machine. Nana died when I was in my twenties. She left notes on every piece of furniture listing who she wanted to have what. "For Laura" was written on the old sewing machine and on all her dining room furniture. I still have all her things.

On my mother's side of the family, Nana was the only great-grandparent I knew growing up. I vaguely remember Poppa, my great-grandfather but he was already very ill when I was a toddler. I knew from a young age that the family was changed forever by the death of the only boy in an entire generation, a beautiful brown hair, blue eyed teenager, my mom's Uncle Billy. Billy was a reconnaissance scout in Patton's 9th armored division and was hit by artillery in Germany four months before the end of the war. He died from his wounds just days before WWII ended. His name is on the WWII memorial in Washington DC. My mom talks to me about it today with the weight of sadness still there after more than 70 years. Nana was never the same again.

Uncle Billy with Nana and Poppa, they were so proud of him

There were strong women in my mother's family. Both her father and her mother had sisters who were always around and part of my mother's life. She was the oldest grandchild by ten years, so she spent much of her childhood around adults. One of her aunts would take her and two younger female cousins into New York City often to see matinees. The outings always started with lunch at white tablecloth Schrafft's Restaurant. My mom laughs and says that her lack of manners was probably embarrassing. In her own home, they never went out to eat, and her mother did not seem interested in teaching Mom any kinds of manners. Years later I would be signed up for cotillion and numerous etiquette classes at our local department store. My mom was determined for us to learn those things. *White Gloves and Party Manners* by Marjabelle Young and Ann Buchwald still sits on my bookshelf today, a cherished Christmas gift in 1965 from my mom. "Hang up clean clothes, place soiled clothes in the laundry basket, use skirt hangers to avoid ugly creases, keep your drawers in order with socks rolled in pairs, arrange your closet sensibly, keep clothes off the floor and polish or clean your shoes twice a week." So many of life's lessons are simple. To this day my mom loves Broadway and pre-Covid she travelled several times a year to see the latest shows. So often we become a reflection of early exposures.

While my mom and dad made it clear that college was the only option for me, my mother's parents made it clear college was not an option for her. My mom was an excellent student, a competitive speaker who competed at the regional and state levels. She graduated from a top Catholic Academy, but her parents saw no value in a girl going to college. They told her it was a waste of money. Instead, after high school she attended the Grace Institute, a secretarial school in the city. Grace offered classes in typing, bookkeeping and stenography so women could take advantage of better paying office jobs in New York City. She was living at home and working to pay for school. Her mother was also charging her for rent and food. She remembers her only plan for the future was to graduate from secretarial school and apply for a good paying job. The only way she was leaving her parents' house was by getting married.

Growing up our home life was very traditional, and, of course, I thought my parents were too strict. We grew up in middle class neighborhoods full of children and moms who stayed home so dads could work long hours. Everyone was after the American Dream. Mom cleaned the house, cooked, and did the laundry; Dad was responsible for the yard. Among the rows of little suburban houses, our yard was always the nicest, and the inside of our house was always clean, too clean. Wednesday was dusting day and Thursday was vacuuming day. I hated it so much as a child. My mom always wanted the house to be perfect. I hated that too. During my whole childhood we had a sofa in the living room that no one was allowed to sit on. My parents worked and saved so long for nice things that they never seemed to enjoy them. If you used them, you would wear them out. Our living room was like a museum and, even in a tiny house, was the room you were not allowed to use. Their house today still has some of the furniture we had growing up. It has now mostly been relegated to guest rooms. The old dining room furniture is now in the kitchen. Their life today looks very different from the outside, but their relationship remains the same. Dad still spends his days working in the yard and tending to his vegetable garden. My mom keeps a spotless house. The old furniture still looks new.

My father had two major roles in life from my viewpoint. One was the times he spent with me in all those simple, pleasant things that fathers do with their daughters — reading, playing at home and going places together as another great adventure with a larger-than-life person who cares about me. The second role was one that I observed and was a more mysterious activity — his dedication to his job and the routine that he followed that was visible to me. He was transmitting something that I did not fully understand but knew was important as well as becoming a formative factor in my later life.

Dad and Me

While I despised all the chores growing up, I developed a respect for the things that I had without realizing it. I swore once I moved away from my parents I would rebel and vacuum once a month and do my wash when I felt like it. It did not work out that way. I grew to understand that they saw their home as a reflection of how much they cared about our family and how appreciative they were of what my father's job had afforded them over the years. They were able to provide a better life than the one provided them as children. They both sacrificed to make a better life, and they were proud of everything they had. To this day they value those old pieces of furniture. They represent the journey, and when my parents are gone, I doubt that I will be able to part with them either. How you care for your things, no matter how much or how little you have, reflects how you care for yourself. People judge us all the time based on what they see, not what they know. When I left for college, I already understood that my future success would be affected by what I was putting out there — how I dressed, how I spoke, how I wrote. The learning curve was long, and it changed from college to career, but I had the foundation. My parents had prepared me to the best of their ability. The rest was up to me.

My father had not just worked hard his entire career, he had mastered being a leader — a manager who developed top sales teams and loyal administrative staffs. His easygoing style and positive attitude masked a driven determination. Always putting in the work so the chance of success was 95%, the chance of failure 5%. To this day he credits his success in all aspects of his life to five simple but meaningful rules by which he has lived. My parents' relationship in all areas of our lives was typical of their time and a bygone era. My dad had the job. He determined where we lived. He managed the money. As a result, he developed the leadership traits that are so admired by everyone in this modern era. Therefore, the results of his character are more obvious. His significant success produced rules for career and life that he promoted and advertised. The five most important are explained below:

1. Always keep your word.

    Your word means more about you than how much money you have, what kind of car you drive or what title you have. His grandfather taught him that the measure of a person is that they will stand behind their promise, their word, their commitment. My dad remembers many business opportunities that came his way because of his reputation for being a man of his word. He may not have made the highest offer but the offer he made and the handshake that backed it up were worth more to the seller. I watched my dad make a deal in the lobby of our office with just a handshake. The business owner drove to Southlake, Texas, from Clarksville, Arkansas, and handed my dad a couple of shoeboxes containing all his customer records, his entire company. My dad shook his hand and said the money would be in his account Monday. It was. There was never any doubt because my dad always kept his word. Keep your word not on just the big things but on the small things. Many people will never know about your business deals, but they will notice that you stop and talk to them, show interest in who they are and fulfill the small promises. I have watched my dad ask our employees if they need anything, just making nice conversation. I recall someone answered jokingly that a new coffee machine would be nice. It was ordered the next day. Always keep your word. He views the customers that way above all else. When customers sign a contract with us, we are giving them our word. Our employees know that we stand behind our word and take responsibility for any mistakes. They operate with the knowledge that the company will always do what is right because there is no other way.

2. Benefit from associating with successful people.

Rarely in life do you try to do something no one has ever tried to do before. Dad calls it copying best practices. Never be afraid to surround yourself or reach out to people who are successful in your industry. Learn through making professional connections — people that are willing to share not just the things that have paid off but also the mistakes. Read about successful people, observe them, study their story. Whatever you are trying to do, chances are there is already someone out there who has tried it. Maybe they succeeded, maybe they failed, but the insight they have gained is invaluable. Lessons learned from mistakes made along the way are as powerful as home runs. Do not fear asking questions or admitting you do not know; share your challenges. Do not be a bragger who always is first with the answer and never with time to listen.

I remember attending an industry convention with my dad. There was a breakfast titled Directory Publishing 101. On stage was a panel of three owners of successful publishing companies. Each had been in the industry for more than 50 years. One was my father. The breakfast was packed, every seat taken. The attendees were given an open mic to ask for guidance and advice on any industry topic. One young publisher in the audience jumped in repeatedly with, "well that didn't work for me, I found a better way." The other 100 members in the room got the message loud and clear; this guy, who only a few people even knew, had all the answers and thought he should be on stage. Ironically the next year he was not at the convention and by the year after that he was out of business. Never be too proud to listen. You may think you know it all, but you do not. Even after a lifetime in the directory publishing business my dad is open to learning new things. He believes in joining professional organizations and being active in industry associations. Absorb new ideas and different ways of doing things. When you are given the opportunity to help another business struggling with issues with which you have dealt, be willing to share your best practices. Surround yourself with successful people and be someone with whom others want to be involved.

3. Do not be afraid of reasonable risk.

Not all risk is a gamble. My dad has lived his life methodically, always doing his homework. He was never the first to do anything; he is not a pioneer. He sits back and watches, until he feels he has considered all angles to the best of his ability. Yes, he has missed out on some opportunities. But I have always believed he had a sixth sense; I realize now it was patience. You must have a decision-making process that you believe in and is comfortable for you, your family, and your financial goals. At different times in our lives, we have responsibilities that dictate the level of risk we can consider. Dad believes that many opportunities will come your way so live life preparing and saving for the right ones. Invest your time in developing connections that can help you make reasoned decisions that cut down the amount of risk when the opportunity knocks. Surround yourself with people whose advice you respect. Dad never stops studying, learning, and observing. Prepare like an athlete. We all fear regret, and risk-taking means the possibility that you may fail. Be realistic about your talents, abilities, and financial situation. Only you can determine when the risk is reasonable for you and your situation. Risk is rarely just about money. It is also about your ego.

4. Every day fix one thing.

It is an incredibly simple concept, fix one thing every day. What it does is train you to plan ahead. In business we like to think big — new products, new strategies, new branding. You do not always have to be looking for big changes to be successful. Consider the small things. There are so many small moving parts that need to work perfectly so the Big gets its Bang. Life is truly a series of small decisions, thus the saying, "it's the little things that count." Getting up every morning with the goal of fixing one small thing, something no one else may even notice, becomes such a motivator. My dad reminded me of this so many times growing up that now it is habit for me. Before I go to bed every night, I inventory the day and map out tomorrow. Most days I fix something very small, even silly — sewing a button on a pair of pants, cutting a small cost by streamlining a process at the office, finishing a project I started but never finished, cleaning off the piles on my desk. When I fix one thing, I give myself credit for a good day; it is a great way to feel good about myself. We love sitting around the conference table and strategizing but when was the last time you asked your team, "What one thing can we fix today?"

5. Respect money.

My dad tells his eight grandchildren that college changed his life, but his respect of money changed theirs. All he saw growing up was the embarrassment caused by not having the money to pay obligations. He watched his parents constantly ask their parents for money because they had overspent. At eleven he would be sent by his parents to the landlord's house all by himself to beg for a few more days to pay the rent. His parents were fine with asking others to make excuses for their money mistakes, but they would not take responsibility themselves. Being late was normal so that made it okay. When my dad served in the Army, he sent his paychecks home to his mom for three years so he would have a nice nest egg when he returned. Unfortunately, when he returned home, most of his money was gone. What hurt him the most was his mother's response when he asked her where his money had gone. "I needed it, so I spent it, I deserved it," she said. Money and the pain it can cause embarrassed my dad as a young child and as a young man returning from war. He decided to be the one who changed.

To this day my dad has pride in the fact that his bills are paid as soon as he receives them. He always keeps track of what he and my mom spend and what bills they have coming in. For him it is about self-respect and pride in your reputation. Some say paying with cash is generational. Today we justify our use of credit by collecting points for status and free stuff that really is not free. How you spend your money is not the issue; it is having respect for your money and the obligations to which you commit that money. Saving is something rarely mentioned. Advertisers realized a long time ago that keeping up with the Jones' was their eureka moment. We judge each other by how we dress, what toys we have, what we drive, and where we live. All the things others can see. My dad believes respecting money comes down to priorities. When he talks about taking reasonable risks and watching people achieve success, the discussion always includes respecting money. Money can do incredible things, but it can also ruin people. Money can bring out the worst and the best. Do not turn away from the mistakes you see family, friends, and businesses make with money. Learn from those mistakes. What started as embarrassment for my father turned into a rule by which he lives. He has shared the good and the bad with my sister, brother and me and with his grandchildren. He feels a strong sense of responsibility to share with us the mistakes made in our own family so that we can make better, more informed decisions. It is his legacy.

Breaking Away

Flipping through the black and white pages of my college yearbooks, I wonder what life has brought these young women, my former classmates. As I reminisce through my four years at a small private women's liberal arts college in the beautiful hills of Virginia, I hope they have achieved their dreams. The college no longer exists as I knew it. In 2007 it become a coed college and was renamed — the only way for it to financially survive. It was founded in 1891 by William Waugh Smith, then President of Randolph-Macon College in Ashland, Virginia. He founded Randolph-Macon Woman's College as "a college where our young women may obtain an education equal to that given in our best colleges for young men and under environments in harmony with the highest ideals of womanhood."

I ended up there quite accidentally. In high school I babysat for neighbors; the woman had graduated from R-MWC in the 60s. She kept her yearbooks on the shelf in the family room and I loved looking at them. The girls were dressed in preppy Dean sweaters and penny loafers. They looked so confident and sophisticated, ready to take on the world. I daydreamed through those pages. I adored the crisp white button-down shirts and tasteful jewelry. I wanted to be one of those confident women. I was determined to go to that college, and I did.

The atmosphere was all about women empowerment back when women empowerment was not discussed. I was an English major, but I took many courses in economics, politics, history, and theatre. I tried everything academically that interested me. Today women's colleges have all but faded. In 1975 there were many choices, all over the country. It was not an obvious choice for me, and I remember my high school counselor was totally dumbfounded by it. I recall one of my male teachers telling me that women's colleges were for girls who only wanted their MRS. degree. I was not changing my mind. I loved the idea of a very small campus, and with boys only around on the weekends, I thought I would do better academically. But it really came down to those pages in my neighbor's yearbook; I was enamored, and I was right.

This past summer I reminisced through those years at R-MWC with my two college roommates. We spent a long weekend on a picturesque lake in Maine. We arrived with old pictures, yearbooks, memories (some foggy) and picked up right where we had left off. We had not all been together in 30 years, but college friendships are like no other. I thought we would be close forever, through thick and thin, but we let life get in the way. All four years in college we were inseparable. How could that change? It crept up on us slowly as the years after college ticked by. We started careers, married, moved to opposite parts of the country, had children, and started new friendships. It seems impossible to consider today, when it is so easy to stay in touch, that in 1979 we depended on snail mail and expensive long distance phone calls.

Valuable friendships deserve your time and effort. I admit the younger me did not understand how much those two women brought to my life. They were my best memories of college. I was not savvy enough to appreciate what I lost when we lost touch. What finally motivated me to track them down and reconnect? The pandemic. I had been on social media for several years and had thought once or twice about looking for them, but I was embarrassed. I felt like a failure for being such a bad friend. I did not know what to say after so many years. What if I found them, messaged them and they didn't respond? I did not want to risk being rejected. We had promised each other that our friendship would last forever.

Fear of the pandemic gripped us in March and April of 2020. What was coming, how bad would it be? I sat in my empty office building; our family business was shutdown. Eight weeks, ten weeks, twelve weeks? No one knew how long the shutdowns would last. Dad and I talked every day. Our priority was paying our employees with no money coming in. But my dad had always planned for the unexpected. 9/11 had slowed our business to almost nothing. From that day my dad started putting company money aside for the unexpected or, heaven forbid, another tragedy. We could assure our employees that we would make it no matter how long it took. My dad never wavered in his positive outlook for our company because he had planned. When he said we would make it, everyone knew we would.

I had that moment of clarity — be positive, have confidence and act now or you will regret it. We often spend too much time worried about what-ifs. Fear of rejection can be paralyzing, but you gain nothing if you make excuses for not trying. These two college friendships were too important to abandon for good. I reached out on Facebook through Messenger. The first messages sat unanswered for a few days; I was disappointed. Then a response! By our second Zoom call we were planning a reunion. In August 2021 we travelled from different parts of the country to a quaint cottage in Maine. For three days we filled it with laughter and tears. We had not grown apart; we were just waiting to continue to grow together.

Friendships are such an important part of college. When my dad took me for my college visits, I knew the moment I saw Main Hall that R-MWC was my place. I felt the history. I was attracted to the intimacy of the small college campus. The student who took us on the tour seemed to know everyone on campus, even professors knew her name and acknowledged Dad and me. I wanted that feeling of belonging, being part of a tight community. A state university was much more affordable, but I was determined and a bit infatuated with the college I had chosen. It meant borrowing money to help with tuition but to me it was worth it. There was something completely different out there, scary in some ways but exciting in others. It was the start of my own adventure, and the beginning of writing my own story. My mom and dad had packed up and started a new life in a place they had chosen; now, I was doing the same thing.

There was a great dynamic on that campus and in the classroom. Older students were encouraged to mentor younger students. Seeing women as leaders in every campus organization was powerful. Even the style of learning had a woman's touch. We would often find spots on the campus grounds to casually gather, discussing assignments or studying for tests. It was not unusual for several of us to go to a professor's house for spirited conversation over dinner or coffee. I had an English professor who hosted a study group for the English majors.

We sat around on the floor of his living room talking for hours about great literature. His apartment was inside a magnificent old mansion with beautiful woodwork, floor to ceiling windows and antique chandeliers. It was a completely different type of discussion setting than I had ever experienced before. It was inspiring. I became very comfortable communicating ideas and debating issues with the other students in this relaxed style. Those experiences helped me develop my casual but effective style of public speaking.

The most challenging classes I took in college were political science. My political science professor pushed hard and relished in the debate when students pushed back. At first, I was too nervous to tell him I did not agree so I sat in class and listened to him shoot down everyone who disagreed. Then I made the mistake of trying to write a paper that mimicked him and not my true beliefs. He gave me a B, noting my arguments lacked moral commitment. Of course, they did, because I was trying to tell him what I thought he wanted to hear. Finally, and I cannot remember the topic, I wrote what I believed and backed it up fully, committing to my position. I got an A, and on my paper, he wrote 'Finally!'

Classes were small; debate was encouraged. He liked stirring the pot. After a particularly heated back and forth, he stopped us and said, "I want to share a story about looking at things through someone else's lens." He told us a story about his dog, a story that had so much hidden value that I have never forgotten it. He had a huge old Bassett hound. One day when he was in the den reading the newspaper, the dog walked in carrying a new bone. The dog walked around every piece of furniture looking for a spot to hide his treasure. He placed it carefully at the base of a chair, and then, making eye contact with my professor, the dog picked up the bone and walked to another spot. Again, the dog looked at my professor, turned and picked up the bone. The dog repeated this several times until he stood looking at the sofa. He made a big jump up on the sofa and set his prize bone on one of the cushions. After he jumped back down, he looked at the sofa — no bone in sight — looked at my professor and walked out of the room, wagging his tail. If he could not see the bone, then my professor could not see it either. His view was the only view he thought mattered.

That really sums up how we all look at things so differently. Twelve women sitting in that classroom all chose the same college, the same class, but we each saw things through our own lens. Our different opinions mirror our different life experiences. It is a valuable lesson because often we do not understand why our family and closest friends do not share our views. There is really nothing to understand; no one walks the same path as anyone else. I learned to appreciate my own experiences and stand up for what I believed but, more importantly, to accept that others would not see things through my lens. You can never be a great leader without learning how to connect in a way that motivates others to give their best while acknowledging their differences.

The theatre taught me how to polish my public presence. My love of drama began later in college after I took a theatre elective to fill a requirement. The theatre professor had a powerful presence; listening to him lecture was almost poetic. I soaked in every word like a sponge. One day after class he asked me why I had waited until my junior year to take a theatre class. He told me I had natural presence, something that could not be taught. That was life changing. I had always preferred to watch rather than participate. His words changed that. I loved being on stage, acting in small roles or building sets. The success of the production was the success of the team. Everyone should experience the challenge of being on stage at least once in their life. I credit it for my ease at public speaking today. To this day I love those first few moments of any public engagement, large or small. Being a successful leader in any setting requires presence and the ability to engage your team. Whenever I have difficult meetings to run or challenging issues to discuss with a group, I go into production mode. Every detail is well planned out — what I wear, if I stand or sit while speaking, do I use a podium or move around the room, am I measured or passionate in my speech?

Women are notoriously tougher on other women than they are on men. I watched the girls who were leaders on campus. They seemed so comfortable in their own skin and worked well with other women. Other women wanted to be around them. Too many women strive to fit in rather than being okay with their uniqueness. We miss opportunities for success, worrying about what others think. Women operate differently, and that is important to understand and accept if your goal is to be a successful leader. It is important to start with yourself. I had big goals for myself, but I kept getting in my own way, wondering how I could be more like others instead of appreciating the skills I had. I cost myself so many opportunities.

Seeing where my path has taken me, it seems odd that I never ran for student government in college. I remember one of the local political clubs contacted me through an upperclassman. They did a sell job on me, told me I would be great for the organization because I had good energy, was well spoken, and excelled in my political science classes. They really built me up, and I remember being so impressed with myself. I guessed they had big plans for me. My first assignment came early one Saturday morning. When I opened the door to my dorm room, there was a box full of political flyers for a man running in the local city election. My first big political assignment was spending my entire weekend walking up and down the streets surrounding the campus putting flyers on people's doorsteps. I was so deflated that by Sunday night my college political career was over. Of course, it is called paying your dues, but I got caught up thinking I was special. I learned that lesson too late for that political club. It is important in the beginning, when joining an organization or starting a new venture, to be willing to do the jobs no one else wants and to do them well, making a name for yourself. When I joined the campus newspaper, I did not make the same mistake; I worked hard and took every assignment. I eventually became a manager, lesson learned:

1. Be reliable. If you say you will do it, do it.

2. Give everything you do your best effort.

3. Be there when you say you are going to be there.

4. Do not miss deadlines.

5. Take responsibility. Do not make excuses.

Those are my strengths to this day.

My college led me to my career in the hotel industry. The whole student body ate meals at the same time in a large dining room. Tables were set with white tablecloths and china bearing the college insignia. Coffee and tea were served with dessert. Student waitresses served food family style on matching China platters. I thought waitressing looked like fun, and it was a job I had excelled at all through high school. I applied for a job but was denied because the positions were reserved for students on work study programs. Rather than accept that, I negotiated my way into a position by offering to be available on call. I handed out flyers at the next few meals to all the regular servers. My promise was to never be late and never miss a shift. Within a few months I was working overtime. That led to a call from the Director of Food Services to serve special dinners hosted by the Dean of the College in the private dining room. Most of the private dinners were for donors. I enjoyed talking to the guests and answering their questions about my experience on campus. I loved the interaction and the pride of serving a beautiful meal on the campus I loved. My supervisor saw my ease at understanding hospitality and offered to set up an internship for me with a member of the community who owned several hotels. I worked the front desk, handled complaints, took reservations, and jumped in to help the restaurant when they were busy. That internship would eventually lead to 14 years in the hospitality industry.

There comes a point in your life, especially for women, when you must make the decision to own who you are. I came out of college realizing all I could be was the best version of myself. I was one of those girls in the yearbook, ready to take on the world in my Dean sweater, crisp white button-down shirt, and tasteful jewelry. I learned that it was up to me to communicate what I wanted in a way that people would listen. Talkers are a dime a dozen; true communicators are very rare. I look at my younger self, and I see the woman I am now; the path was not always smooth, but I came out of college ready to fight for the woman I would ultimately become. My parents had worked hard and saved money so college would be a guarantee, not a possibility, for me and my siblings. When I was graduating, my sister was finishing her freshman year. My dad had honored the man who he respected the most, his grandfather.

1979, Randolph-Macon Woman's College

Mom and Dad expected me to have a good job lined up by graduation day. During my last semester I got on a plane for only the second time in my life and flew to Ohio for a day-long interview in Solon with Stouffer Hotels. I was thrilled when the job offer came to join their management team. The management training program would not start until two months after college graduation. I was looking forward to some down time. My dad's first question was, "What do you plan on doing for money between graduation and your first paycheck?" There went my vacation. I applied with a temp agency the next Monday and worked 8-5 every day for eight weeks until my plane left for Dayton, Ohio. There was not going to be any down time for me.

Many years later, I was passing through Lynchburg and stopped to visit my college campus. It was summertime so everything was locked up. I spent an hour walking the beautiful campus reminiscing. There was a security guard on the grounds, and I waved and went over to introduce myself. I asked if there was any way he could show me my old room in Main Hall. Together we walked up the grand staircase, made a right turn through the study area, and there was my college dorm room, frozen in time. He was kind enough to step back and let me feel that moment. It was very emotional. College opened doors for me; it raised my confidence and taught me how to speak up.

LEARNING FROM BOSSES — GOOD AND BAD

It was a culture shock leaving a small women's college and starting a career in a totally male-dominated industry. I never gave it a thought when I was interviewing. Not that it would have made a difference; I needed a good job. My first management job paid $13,000 a year. Everyone I reported to, all the way up to Hotel General Manager, was a man. I was not concerned about holding my own, but I was surprised how much I missed having women from whom to learn and aspire. I missed the female leadership of the upperclassmen I had looked up to in college, and I missed mentoring younger classmates as I had when I became a junior and senior. I would soon discover that my biggest challenge would be becoming part of the 'club.'

My first job after the training program was Assistant Restaurant Manager at Stouffer's Cincinnati hotel, managing the graveyard shift in their 24-hour restaurant. How do you get ahead when your boss rarely sees you? I started my shift at 9pm, and I finished at 6am. I found out later it was the number one job in the company no one wanted. I poured coffee, cleared tables, buttered toast, washed dishes and mopped the kitchen floor. You realize very quickly the importance of a dishwasher when one quits in the middle of a busy shift, or how much a hostess hustles when yours calls in sick. I learned many important things from the employees. I learned what it feels like to be low man on the totem pole. I learned that working as hard as your employees not only sets a great example, but it builds trust and loyalty. My employees showed up for me. It was an awful shift to find great employees, but we built a team that watched out for each other. The customers and the hotel benefitted.

One of the keys to effective leadership is to unlock other people's potential by making them feel valued. People spend too much time trying to develop their own management style; the key is the style of the people who work for you. At that hotel it was not about title or position; I wore a name tag that said Manager, but that did not mean much when there were 60 people waiting in line to be seated. I was 22 years old and thought that if you sat in a big executive office with many people reporting to you, you must be a leader. It is ironic, looking back, but I worked in that hotel for 18 months and I never met the general manager. He made no effort to meet his manager at the bottom of the totem pole, the one making sure all his customers were taken care of at 2am. That made a lasting impression on me. That job taught me that there are many people with impressive titles that do not lead, and many people with no title at all that lead every day.

My hours were also the opposite of my immediate boss, so we rarely saw each other. He managed me by leaving me notes with the dinner hostess. After almost two months without talking to him in person, I called him and set up a breakfast meeting. I realized that to get ahead I needed him to be invested in my career. I was willing to do the hard work, but I needed to get my successes in front of the people who mattered. I asked him to come in every two weeks and have breakfast with me after my shift. I invited other mangers in the hotel to stop by for a meal before or after their shifts — my treat. I went from being 'the poor manager of the graveyard shift' to someone everyone knew. I created a support system where none had been. Over time I realized that my system had a downside. My boss had no interest in me transferring; I had made myself irreplaceable in a job no one wanted. It was up to me to identify and train my replacement and then show my boss that she was perfect for the job. A year later I was promoted, and I arrived at my new hotel in Valley Forge, Pennsylvania, looking for my replacement on day one.

Feeling confident after my first promotion, I was ready for another success. Unfortunately, I ran into a bulldozer. We have all met people who are impossible to please. Most of them we run from but what do you do when that person is your boss? How do you work around them to reach your goals? My only experience so far in my career had been with bosses who wanted me to succeed. This man wanted me to fail. Finally, home after an exhausting 14-hour shift, he called me to yell at me because the kitchen floor had not been mopped completely. He told me if I could not manage the staff, he would find someone who could. It was all I could do not to burst into tears. Instead, I listened silently, calling him an ass in my head. Then I picked up the phone and called the one person I knew would sympathize with me, my dad. I tearfully shared my outrage and how much I hated my boss and then announced that I was going into work the next day and quitting.

After I finally took a breath, my dad said, "No, you are not quitting; you are getting in your car right now and going back to the hotel to mop the floor yourself. You made a mistake; you forgot that your employees had a long, hard day too, and you didn't check to make sure their work was done. You hate your boss? Then do the job better than any other manager in that hotel and earn his respect." By the next morning word that I had come in at midnight and mopped the floors myself spread like wildfire through the hotel. I sat down with my employees, and we set standards to which everyone agreed so small jobs would not fall through the cracks. I stepped into the leadership role by taking responsibility rather than blaming my staff. More importantly, I learned how crucial respect is to leadership and success. My boss was still difficult and never missed a chance to be critical until the day I got a better offer. The hotel's general manager had left a few months after mop-gate to take a job with a new hotel company. I may not have impressed my immediate boss, but that general manager felt differently. I remember getting the phone call and a nice offer to join the staff of his new hotel. The offer was one I had to consider so I told my boss what was going on. He was only upset that the former GM was trying to steal one of 'his' managers. He stormed off to complain to the new general manager. The next day there was a dramatic change in my boss. I was asked to stay. I received a raise and flowers were delivered to me at the restaurant. I had followed my father's advice; my boss may not have valued my work but the executives at the top did.

I am amazed that so many of my bosses did not see the value in mentoring younger managers as part of their own success strategy. I worked for some very talented people along the way, but I could tell who was on the fast track to success, and who was on the way out. My next boss was a man on the fast track; he was smart, organized, and oozed 'company man.' He was the perfect manager from whom to watch and learn until I figured out that he was not teaching me, he was timing me. He valued the hours his team worked more than what they accomplished during those hours. It was interesting because that was how he operated himself. He did not care what time his boss came in; he was going to beat him. He was the first to arrive and the last to leave, and if you left before him, he always had a subtle comment. This was a man who had a wife and children waiting at home. I was single, lived in a studio apartment, and did not even have a pet fish. I felt I had no choice but to play the game, so I started coming in earlier and staying later. I noticed that he responded to that. He would come looking for me in the restaurant, have a cup of coffee and make comments like, "Wow, you're still here."

After a few months I decided not to play the game anymore; I was wasting so much time. When my annual review came, he was very happy with my job performance. He was happier, however, with the 10- to 12-hour days I was working. I finally asked, "Why is it so important that I put in a longer day than you do? I'm wasting time, my job is done, and I've trained my assistant managers. They do a great job, but the message I am sending them is that I don't have confidence in them. You make me feel the same way." He did not agree with my point of view. Somewhere along his own career path he had been taught that hours prove your level of dedication to the job, and he was not going to change. While we did not agree, it was a great lesson that became part of my management style. I see no value in time for the sake of time. Do the job as efficiently as you can, and measure your success by results, not hours.

Tempers were something you accepted in the stressful world of food service. It was unfortunately common for arguments to happen during busy service times. I remember losing my temper and yelling at a waitress in the middle of a breakfast rush. She was having a meltdown in the kitchen, and everyone was trying to help her. She could not remember where anything went. Customers were complaining so I went back in the kitchen to find out what was going on. I lost my cool and made the situation ten times worse. She walked out. I deserved it. We barely made it through that shift. It was uncomfortable for me with my staff; they were disappointed in me. It took a couple of days for me to apologize. I did not want to be that kind of manager, but I resented the fact that male managers and chefs could yell, and no one thought twice. Whether I liked it or not, I was judged more harshly because I was a woman. I was still wrong. I learned the value of making a heart-felt apology to your team when you let them and yourself down. It had cost me some trust and some respect, and I had to accept that and fix it. I learned that things are not always fair but doing the right thing is more important than fairness.

My next transfer would be at my request. I was getting married and moving to California where my fiancé was stationed at George Air Force Base in the Mojave Desert. We met in college on a blind date. Determined to make it work long distance after college without Zoom, Facetime or even text, we spent a fortune on phone bills and plane tickets. A year out of college we got engaged and immediately he decided to join the Air Force. We survived officer training school and flight training school. Once he got his first assignment, I was ready to visit his base and experience military life. It did not go well. I remember the squadron wives were so welcoming. They invited me to a Tupperware party (my first and only), followed by a macramé party (my first and last). Many already had babies and young toddlers. I knew I could not do it. I had made my decision by the time I got on the plane back home. We were both 23 years old and headed in different directions, dreaming completely different dreams. We chose career over marriage and ended our engagement. He went on to serve our country overseas, and I concentrated on my next promotion. Almost five years went by, and we had lost touch when out of the clear blue sky my 'almost' mother-in-law called. She was excited to tell me that my former fiancé was moving back to the United States. That phone call led to a call a few weeks later from him. After a few months of dating by phone I flew out to California where he was stationed. I came home with my old engagement ring back on my finger and a request to transfer. We were married the next year.

My years of hard work paid off with a transfer to the company's new hotel opening at the Los Angeles Airport. It was the largest hotel I had ever helped open, 750 rooms. I came with a great resume and many successes. I had become someone the company tapped for opening new hotels, and I had just returned from a three-month assignment opening a hotel at the Denver airport. I had developed a great reputation for training employees and building successful teams. The Los Angeles hotel had hired a group of impressive managers, many with long careers in the hotel industry. It would be a chance to observe and learn from some of the most professional managers with whom I would ever work. My skills were needed and appreciated but I knew I was learning more from them than they were from me.

Another valuable lesson. Never pass up a chance to work with the best in your field. I made the most of every day; it was an incredible learning experience that I still benefit from today.

Once the Los Angeles hotel was open and operating smoothly, I started to think hard about the commitment needed to continue to climb the corporate ladder in such a time demanding industry. Working long hours, weekends, and holidays when I was single was one thing but now, I was married, and I wanted to be a mom. I was smart enough to know that between the hours and the long commute, something would have to give. I never considered that children would affect my career in any way that was not manageable. More women were joining the workforce, and I was able to see how other moms were able to juggle kids and career. I was sure things would work out on my schedule, but I was wrong. We lost our first pregnancy, something I never considered could happen to me. How could it happen to me? I still have my tonsils. I was surrounded by so many pregnant wives in the squadron that I could not get away from babies, baby showers and the constant chatter about trimesters. We were determined that as soon as it was okay, we would try again. I buried myself in my job and counted the months. One year later our daughter was born, and I left the career I loved and the company I respected. I was grateful that I could make the right decision for myself and my family. Moving forward our transfers would be in the hands of the US Air Force. I knew I would figure out a way to continue my career; I had invested too much of myself. It did not take long before my husband received his new assignment. Baby (and dog) in tow, we packed up and headed to the Last Frontier.

The Last Frontier

There are living room women and kitchen women. Living room women always seem to have it together. There is something cool about them. Their makeup and hair are always perfect; their calendars are full of lunches and coffee with the girls. People like knowing them. They seem to move seamlessly through life. I am a kitchen woman. Everything gets done but it is never pretty. I only have a few close friends. If my hair looks great, I just came from the hairdresser. At the end of each day, I sit on the sofa and kick up my feet, proud of myself for somehow getting it all done (well almost all of it). Moving to Alaska was landing in my kindred kitchen world. The extreme weather had no appreciation for dressing up and perfect hair. If I ever had any hope of someday being a living room woman, Alaska dashed my hopes forever. It was a shocking change from Los Angeles in every way. I loved being okay with looking okay. Hair cannot look anything but electrified after pulling off a wool hat, so embrace the ponytail. Alaska taught me to celebrate shortcuts and simplify wherever you can. I live by that to this day.

According to my plan, Alaska would be a two-year detour. I was in no rush to get back in the workforce, especially when it was not an investment in the career waiting for me in the lower 48. It was the perfect time to stay home with my daughter. Nothing could have prepared me for how much time I would spend alone. Our husbands were assigned 'TDY' temporary duty for weeks at a time. The wives formed a tight-knit group, shoring each other up through the loneliness — casseroles and toddlers in tow. Alaska has reported three times when temperatures hit -70 degrees, spells that last two or three days. Those three times were January 1952, 1975, and 1989. I spent the whole month of January 1989 locked up in the house alone with an 11 month old and our family dog. It was the icicle that broke the moose's back. I made the decision to find a job as soon as the snow started to thaw.

It was emotional walking into the lobby of an unfamiliar hotel. I felt like I was the new kid on the first day of school. I almost turned around. If I was going to take a break from the company I loved, maybe I should try a whole new field. It was Alaska after all; I could do something in tourism, maybe something outdoors. But I kept looking at my resume; it was super strong, and this hotel gig would be a sure thing. I did not want to add more to what was already monumental change. I dropped my resume at the front desk. I remember that the young man whose name badge said Assistant Front Desk Manager smiled politely and told me they were not hiring but he would pass my resume on to HR. It was early March, the tourist season was still a few months away, and businesses were just starting to come out of hibernation. I was relieved; maybe I would try the other big hotel in Anchorage, but why bother as it would probably be the same story. I would wait until May and try again. I had just crossed the street when I heard a woman calling my name. When I turned around, I saw a woman running toward me with my resume waving in her hand. I knew I was hired. She introduced herself as the HR Director and asked if I would have time to meet with the hotel's General Manager. I started at the Sheraton Anchorage Hotel the next week.

The best laid plans rarely work out. Alaska was a two-year military assignment. Then my husband would put in for a transfer, moving us back to a base in the lower 48 where I could rejoin my old company. But while we were in Alaska, Operation Desert Shield became Operation Desert Storm. The Air Force froze every Officer in the squadron. Two years turned into almost five. I would finally start to feel connected to a place and put down some roots. Ironically, it was in a place that never fit in to my plan.

I walked into the hotel the first morning feeling overconfident and cocky. I had worked at some incredible hotels, opened hotels in Rochester, Denver, and Los Angeles. I had made so many business connections over the years and had colleagues working all over the United States and other parts of the world. I was part of an informal hospitality network, professionals that I could call for anything. I loved being in the know, hearing the gossip, being asked for advice and guidance, so working at a midsize older hotel in Anchorage, Alaska, would be a piece of cake. Or so my ego told me. Everyone I had worked with over the years was excited to hear about living in Alaska, and that first summer I had great tales to tell. But Alaska has another side and soon I would learn a valuable lesson; do not let your ego get in the way of a good learning experience.

Our first summer was glorious. Alaska is National Geographic come alive. I remember so many mornings opening the blinds and being face-to-face with a huge momma and baby moose happily eating our bushes. The drive to work was a gorgeous windy road from Eagle River into the city. Everything was deep green, flower baskets hung from every porch and gardens burst with color. Summer meant sunshine almost 24 hours a day. Neighbors would cut their lawn or wash their car at 10pm. Weekends were nonstop. I had never been an outdoor girl but that all changed in Alaska. It was intoxicating — hiking in the nearby Chugach Forest or along the glacier at Alyeska. We spent hours in hip waders fly fishing on the Kenai. Alaska has more landing strips than any other state. My husband had his private pilot's license, and the Air Force base rented planes at a reasonable cost. We would fly to Talkeetna at the foot of Mount Denali for lunch and spend the afternoon hiking in Denali National Park. The animals were everywhere you looked — black bears, moose, bald eagles, and Dall sheep hugging the mountainside. If you headed down to the Kenai early in the morning, you might be able to experience the bore tide coming into the Cook Inlet; it sounds like a train barreling down the tracks — a wall of water six feet tall in places, moving like a controlled tidal wave. There were mountain goats, puffins, and ptarmigans. The Air Force base had a bald eagle sanctuary for wounded eagles. We had four incredible summers in Alaska where I discovered my love of fishing and my appreciation for our national park system. I developed a deep respect for nature and a healthy caution when you are in its home. Beware of the bears was a common sign around our neighborhood at the foot of Chugach State Park.

The hotel buzzed with activity during that first summer. Tourists packed the lobby, excited to start their wilderness adventure. There was a fine dining restaurant on the top floor of the hotel. On a clear day you could see Mount Denali in one direction and the Cook Inlet in the other. Dinner reservations were at a premium because you could enjoy the view no matter how late you ate. Every day was a postcard. June, July, and August tourists paid top dollar to visit a place I was lucky enough to call home. The days were so long during the summer that after work you still had time to hike or go canoeing. Vendors that offered guided tours had desks throughout the hotel lobby and early in the season invited the hotel managers to take their tours so we would recommend them. There was so much energy, but it was a rugged energy. Boots were the only shoe, summer or winter.

Many say Alaska is a state of two seasons. Winter and June, July and August. You feel the shift — first the tourists leave, then the sun. Gradually the cold moves in to take its place until March. Operating in a city shifting from light to dark, warm to frigid, affects your psyche. Managing a staff through frozen dark days with only hazy sunlight was challenging. The palpable energy in the hotel during the summer gave way to quiet. Weather was the hurdle. Snow was constant from October to March. I always pictured one huge snowstorm that blanketed everything, and then constant flurries for months. It ebbed and flowed, some days with small flurries, then big snowstorms would roll in making it impossible for the early morning shift to get in until the streets were cleared. We watched the weather constantly, stressing over opening the restaurant on time for our hotel guests. There was some of that same loneliness I felt when I was the overnight manager in Cincinnati, when it is 5am and you are praying for a cook to arrive.

Building a team is great, but if your team members are snowed in, all the spirit in the world will not drive them to work. It is the same with any big task. Your team may have great training, and they may be raring to go but does the plan hold up when the unexpected happens. I had heard the horror stories, the mornings no one could get in. It did not happen often. Anchorage is certainly prepared for snowstorms, but there is snow and then there is SNOW. The worst were the storms that started well after midnight, filling the roads with a wall of white, making it impossible for the 5am shift to get to work on time. My first winter in Alaska was tough, but I pulled the team members together, wait staff, kitchen staff, dishwashers, and management, and I asked each shift the same question. What would you do if you were here all alone at 5am and knew you had to open the doors at 6am? They came up with multiple 'what if' plans. They tapped into the other departments who were already in the hotel overnight. When we knew a big storm was forecast, I would spend the night in the hotel along with our executive chef. Employees that lived downtown offered to be part of an emergency call list. They came up with a very basic breakfast option for guests that required having products on hand for a ready-to-go option. Their 'worst scenario' plan was tested more than once. Chef and I were relieved to report that their plan worked. I started our meeting with one goal-oriented question: How do we serve our guests if you cannot make it in? The employees began to think of their contribution and how their job could be done more efficiently. It really brought the team together with an appreciation of each contribution. It also streamlined our existing 'summertime' processes so year-round we became more efficient. We did not need to operate seasonally, we needed to operate smarter. To this day I start every meeting with a goal-oriented question.

There are some things for which you cannot plan, but if you have basic emergency procedures in place, it is a great deal easier. Unless of course you are in Anchorage during a volcanic rain. Who had ever heard of volcanic rain, much less prepared to manage a staff through it? In August of 1992 with a sold-out hotel full of tourists, a huge black ash cloud 30 miles wide covered the entire city. Mount Spurr, about 80 miles west of Anchorage, had erupted, hurling ash 10 miles into the sky. The city turned completely dark. By 5:30pm we knew the cloud was coming our way. The immediate issue was to get everyone inside and safe. Then we went into power mode to keep the ash out and get everything we could covered in the hotel. We pulled huge linen carts from housekeeping filled with sheets and towels, and teams went through the administrative offices covering the computers. Other teams went into our kitchens covering all machines, cash registers, and appliances. We had a few hours' notice, so we pulled everyone on property together in the lobby. We sent teams out with specific tasks. Hotel maintenance covered outside air ducts and doorways, anything they could do to keep the fine ash out. By 8:30pm that night the ash fell. You could hear the strangest hissing sound in the darkness and the wind picked up, swirling the dust like mini tornadoes. Streets were coated in a quarter inch of gray dust; cars that had ventured out rushed to find cover. I have never experienced anything close to that since. The city was covered for weeks, and when it rained, the ash turned into an awful pasty sludge and the smell of sulfur filled the air. We may not have had a plan for volcanic rain, but we had an emergency plan that only took a bit of creative thinking to implement and protect the hotel and our guests.

My management style seemed to work better in Alaska. I had always been a bit of a bull in the china shop. I had wasted time as a young manager trying to copy people I could never be. Alaska appreciated toughness. I was also getting older and with that came the mellowing of my intensity. I realized that being a tough female manager was and should be okay if done with fairness and consistency. When the team succeeded, I succeeded and if I always remembered to share the stage with them, we would be successful at anything into which we put our effort. I was putting down roots for the first time. I was no longer obsessed with my next transfer because there was nowhere to go. I found myself setting goals for next year, not just next month. This job I thought would be temporary had turned into a continuation of the career I thought I had left behind.

As much as I hated always being the new kid growing up, I had gone through the process so many times that I learned a few tricks. A new job takes a year to settle in — period. Be prepared to heavily invest your time and effort in the first year of any new undertaking. Developing relationships and becoming a connector are key and that takes time and strategic thinking. Years earlier opening a new hotel in New York, I worked with a manager who was masterful at making client connections. People wanted to do business with him. He moved into the community and chose to embrace it. He became involved in philanthropy and community service; he made connections that had value. It was so much deeper than networking, having a few drinks, a few lunches. He developed bonds over shared causes. Those types of connections form meaningful relationships that easily turn into business. I watched and learned from him, and it paid off when my job and love of politics crossed paths.

Military bases are very tight knit communities. In Alaska every family serving was far away from home. I had never missed a family Thanksgiving or Christmas, and it was especially hard having the only grandchild in our family. But between bad weather and distance, we missed many holidays back home. Our friends in the squadron became like family — potlucks, fishing trips, cross stitch, sharing sour dough starter and favorite crock pot recipes. Girls' trips were deep sea halibut fishing or camping along the Kenai. Being in a squadron is incredibly special. To this day I have never experienced camaraderie like that. We had to count on each other because we were all far from family and our husbands travelled so much. If your heater broke on a frigid Alaska night and your husband was away, you just called another squadron family. If you had a sick child, squadron friends would come right away to help you. It taught me so much about being a reliable friend. To this day if a friend needs my help, I rearrange whatever I am doing to help them.

I was one of very few wives who worked outside of the home. Military life for spouses when you are moving every two years, raising small children, and picking up and packing up is hard. It does not leave much time to have a meaningful career or friendships outside of the squadron. I was proud of my position at the hotel. It required a great deal of juggling, but we made it work. When my husband was travelling, I would bring our daughter to the hotel with me while I checked on evening events. Chef would make her a bowl of pasta, and she would sit at the big table in his office while I worked the ballroom making sure my clients were happy. Weekdays my husband would drop her at the base daycare and pick her up on his way home. I remember her caregiver telling my husband that the children had talked about what their mom and dad did at work, and our daughter announced that her mom went to parties all the time! The next time I took her to the hotel I showed her the big banquet rooms, kitchens and restaurants and explained what my job was.

One of my favorite memories was a huge lunch for 500 guests hosted at the hotel. Security was all over the hotel. Secretary Dick Cheney was the honored guest speaker. Cheney was serving as Secretary of Defense for President George H. W. Bush; his speech was incredible. The event was a who's who of Alaska business, military, civic and political dignitaries. When Cheney finished, the entire room stood, giving him a rousing standing ovation. Security had made prior arrangements to bring Secretary Cheney through the banquet kitchen to the service elevator after his speech. Chef and I had our staff lined up in the kitchen as he was escorted through. I remember Secretary Cheney looking at the line of servers, cooks, dishwashers, sous chefs and catering managers and raising his hand slightly to signal his security that he wanted to stop. He stood in front of our entire staff and thanked them for their luncheon service and said his filet was cooked perfectly. He stopped in front of the Executive Chef and me and thanked us both by name and shook our hands. That meant the world to each employee and was obviously a moment I never forgot. It was especially meaningful for me, a military spouse. A man that would go on to be Vice President of the United States, a politician operating in rarefied air had taken the time to make us, the little guys, feel appreciated for a job well done. There is a valuable leadership lesson there. Never think you are too big to acknowledge a job well done and always take the time to say thank you.

I was proud to be a military wife and Alaska was a place that really held the military in high regard. Because of my position as food and beverage director, I often interacted with military leadership and their aides through events hosted at the hotel or catered by the hotel on base. I had the honor of meeting both Commanding Officers of Alaska Air Command, General Thomas McInerney and General Joseph Ralston. They were military royalty and for those of us whose husbands were Lieutenants, Captains, or Majors, we were star struck. I remember a special family event the squadron attended on base. General Ralston arrived and a murmur went through the room; all the officers straightened. He walked into the room and every officer stood and saluted. As he moved through the hangar he smiled, nodding to everyone with a polite hello. When he got to my husband and me, he stopped. He reached out his hand to shake mine and addressed me by name. He asked how I was doing and thanked me for the lovely job the hotel had done recently at an event hosted at his home. All eyes in the squadron were on me. No one seemed to breathe for those few seconds. My husband was pretty stunned too.

My position at the hotel afforded me the opportunity to meet all the local and state political representatives and their staffs. The hotel was where numerous galas, fundraisers and political rallies were hosted. In my position, I was the contact for all the political events. It was my first opportunity to meet a US Congressman, Don Young, who served the people of Alaska until his death in 2022. I loved working with our local government officials and watching how they operated in large social settings. Organizing and managing events came naturally to me, but I felt a special sense of excitement and anticipation during political events. I listened to the speakers from the back of the room so I could watch the reaction of the guests. The great speakers had a natural presence that held the room; you could see guests nodding in agreement and clapping at the appropriate times. I loved the buzz that was always around the special ones, and it really ignited my passion for politics. Public speaking is so important to how people judge you and respond to you. It can be a small group or a large group but how you present your words is as important as what you are saying.

I think we would have been happy if we had retired from the military and stayed in Alaska forever. It suited us perfectly. My husband loved the outdoors, hunting for moose and caribou, fishing for silver salmon "silvers" in the Russian River or king salmon along the Kenai River south of Anchorage. I was never an outdoor type, but I loved to fish with him and our daughter. We slept in tents, yurts, and RVs; things I had never done before. Alaska was all about the great outdoors, enjoying nature, and pushing yourself to try new things. Our garage was full of outdoor gear — an inflatable fishing boat my husband shared with two other squadron members, rubber waders of various lengths hanging from the ceiling alongside fishing nets of all sizes. Fishing poles lined the walls. I found out I was pregnant with our second child during caribou season in 1992. My husband had gone hunting over the weekend and shot a big caribou buck. He brought it home and had it in the garage while he was preparing the meat for the packaging plant and the head for the taxidermist. I opened the garage door, took one look, and proceeded to throw up not once, not twice, but for hours. Turns out I was pregnant.

That next year, our tour in Alaska finally came to an end when the military assigned us to Langley Air Force Base in Hampton, Virginia. It would be my husband's first desk job which meant pushing paper and not flying. Our son was born two months before we left for the new assignment. Once again, the timing was perfect for my career. Leaving was hard but to this day I appreciate every moment I experienced in that magical place. I walked into that Anchorage hotel overconfident and cocky. I believed they were lucky to have me; I was the lucky one. If you think you are overqualified for a position then you are probably unwilling to learn and consider new ways of doing things. Take off the shades. Confidence is a positive trait but confidence must be kept in check constantly; there is no kicking back and gliding if you want people to respect you and do a great job for you.

In June 1993 we packed up two little ones, the dog, and all our outdoor memories and left Alaska on a beautiful summer morning. We knew what we were losing — a lifestyle we would never experience again. For the first time in our married life, we would not be part of a squadron and knew we would miss the close-knit friendships it provided. This next home needed to fill a big void. We had gotten into an ebb and flow that worked for us; this move would be a huge disruption in more ways than we could have imagined.

THERE WILL BE DISAPPOINTMENTS

I do not ever remember walking into a new school and making a great friend on the first day, like you see on TV. I was the new kid for what seemed like months. It was always a scary time as a kid; high expectations for the first day followed by disappointment. It always worked out but waiting to meet that first friend seemed to take forever. Physically I was gawky, always the tallest and skinniest, which I hated. One of my earliest disputes was in the first grade with a girl who lived in my neighborhood. She constantly called me Downey duck legs!! I guess ducks have boney legs and Downey was my last name. One day I pushed back and called her fatso the cat. (Her last name was Sylvester, so it made sense to me.) That was my first lesson that all insults are not equal. She ran home in tears. Our doorbell rang within minutes; it was her mom. She wanted to let my mom know what a mean name I had called her daughter. When my mom replied that the name calling went both ways and that calling me duck legs was not nice either, the mother replied that you cannot compare the two. My mom stood up for me, but I still got a lecture after the front door closed and another one when my dad got home. Isn't mean just mean?

Do not be afraid to let your children be disappointed. Learning to handle disappointments at a young age will pay off in the type of successes they try to attain. They will not see limitations as insurmountable, and they will not be as afraid to face the heartbreak of failure. Parents are a child's first mentors; they can teach positive lessons that will help their child succeed or teach their child to blame others when things do not go their way. You will make life easier for them in the workforce if you teach them to value advice and guidance from respected adults in their lives. They will be more apt to reach out and establish positive mentor relationships. No boss will love your child like you do so do not raise them to expect others to cater to their needs.

Childhood disappointments are necessary, and some stay in your heart for a very long time. They teach you empathy and empower you to take risks. To this day I can tell the story of trying out for our high school cheerleading squad as if it had happened last week. I have told my children the story over the years in hopes of teaching them about disappointment. I still tell it with so much painful emotion that my children feel sympathy for me. My youngest asked me to please not tell it anymore. I can only imagine how it hurt 49 years ago if I still cringe today. I tried out twice. I did not make it, twice. Those were the days when the results were posted on the front door of the school. Can you imagine? All the girls rushed off the bus and gathered around the handwritten list. I had practiced for weeks in front of the bathroom mirror, in front of my sister, my dog Shannon, and the girls on my street. At tryouts I was nervous, but I jumped around with lots of energy and my signature loud voice. My neighborhood friends who were there trying out said I did great; my cartwheel and back walkover were perfect.

Jumping off the bus that next day I was elated. I was sure I had made it; there was no doubt in my mind it was my big break. It was so much more than cheerleading to me. I was entering the 10th grade in a brand-new school, and I was desperate to fit in, maybe even be one of the popular girls. Our family had moved so much over the years that I always felt sure I would have had many friends if only I had more time. I quickly scanned the list, excited to spot my name. When it was not in the Ds where it should have been alphabetically, I jumped to the Ls assuming an oversight. Girls around me started screaming with joy, others broke away and wandered quietly down the hallway. The girls that lived on my street ran over and grabbed me screaming, did you make it? Before I could even answer, other girls circled in jumping up and down, hugging and laughing and gradually pushing me out of this new inner circle. I kept trying to strain over the heads to see the list, maybe I just missed my name. I was devastated and cried for days. I can remember going to the grocery store with my mother after school and refusing to come in. I just lay on the backseat of the car and cried.

My parents handled it the right way although I cannot imagine how they felt watching my three-day meltdown. They acknowledged my disappointment, even while I blamed them for making us move in the first place. When I insisted that I deserved a spot, they did not agree. Nobody told me I was right, the judges were wrong, the system was rigged. They did not buy me presents to make me feel better. They told me I would feel better, and I could try again. I did feel better eventually, and I did try again the next year. If you think the experience could not have been worse, you would be wrong. The second time I froze when they called my name. I cannot remember doing my cheer routine, but somehow after my cartwheel I ended up flat on my back. How I got there, I will never know. It was not meant to be, no reason to check the list.

Certainly, cheerleading tryouts were not my only disappointment growing up, but the experience set the bar high for risks I was willing to take. Failure and embarrassment in front of your peers can be especially painful; no matter what your age. I would never have had the guts to run for elected office or for board chairman of a national association. I would not have had the confidence to put myself in a public position where I could lose. My disappointments have helped me be a more empathetic leader. After freezing during 11th grade cheer tryouts, the coach pulled me aside the next day. She acknowledged my disappointment, but she told me that she recognized my determination and willingness to keep trying. I had handled the disaster with grace. So much of growing up is learning to handle embarrassment and disappointment. What happened to me has happened to others in thousands of different pressure situations. What a huge impact the coach made on me by seeking me out and taking the time to mentor me in that moment. Over the years I have had great women teachers who took the time to reach out to me; they were planting the seeds of mentoring.

Many generations of women fought for the empowerment we enjoy today. Yes, there is still much to be done and it starts with each of us. Women must be the biggest cheerleaders for other women. We must lift other women up by recognizing their achievements. Be there with a compliment, not judgment. Mentoring other women is so important to the future accomplishments for which we all strive. It is still a battle for women to get to the top but when we do, we must reach down to pull other women up with us. Unfortunately, once we fight our way to the top, we often hunker down protecting our turf. It is up to us to mentor the next generation of girls. Our responsibility is to make their path smoother with our guidance.

Once I managed a restaurant and bar with four male assistant managers. One of my assistants was promoted and transferred to another company property. We were excited for him and excited to find out who his replacement would be. The waiting turned into a month and still no word on who our new assistant would be. The managers were getting a bit frustrated having to cover the extra shifts. We were in a staff meeting and someone asked, "Why is it taking so long to find a new manager?" One of the male managers jumped in immediately stating as fact that women are hard to work for and maybe that was why it was taking so long. He was very pointed about it, like it was a perfectly normal thing to consider. I was speechless but acted like I did not hear him. It still goes on today. It is just a little more hush hush.

Throughout my hotel career I had the opportunity to work for managers with very different styles. One new person above you or below you can change the direction of an effective team. Do not ever let a new team member step in and take root without your counsel. Whether it is a new boss or a new employee, sit down and get to know them, offer your time, and find out their goals. I have worked for managers who were obvious about their ambition to move up. I have also worked with managers who wanted my job. But in each case, I made sure I understood the reality of the situation. My concern was how it affected the team. It was important to fit new members of the team into the process that was working but acknowledge their goals and make sure that they were invited to contribute. It is important that each team member's goals are constantly reevaluated and that the way you operate is open to changes agreed upon by the team. Meaningful communication cannot be saved for annual reviews. Some employees are very open about their goals, some claim to not have any, and some need help developing them. Make yourself available as a mentor by showing ongoing interest in each employee's goals. A great manager organizes the team first with good processes that ensure a blueprint for success.

I have had bosses hand me books on effective management styles. I read a few; none really spoke to me. Too many people get caught up in developing their perfect management style. What makes your team members perform is more important than what makes you perform. So many things can change the dynamic so you must be nimble. Highlight your strengths and build a management strategy around them but invest time in discovering what motivates those you are trying to lead. Your style must be flexible because a new boss can reshuffle priorities in 24 hours. It is important to find out what motivates your team members, and then you need to become that leader. You do not have to change your personality or your values. Great leadership is not about personality as much as it is about process.

I remember watching the downfall of one of my bosses. I was a midlevel manager with a couple of assistant managers reporting to me. My boss was more interested in being social than in being the boss. It did not matter how busy or shorthanded we were, he never lent a hand. He was either in his office or holding court in the lobby bar, drinking, and telling stories with the male managers. I was never invited. I am sure I would have been a downer, but I resented being left out. I admit I never went to him for guidance. I saw him as a slacker, but my peers saw him as fun. He was always in a great mood; he had no expectations of his team which endeared him to almost everyone. He told me my first day, "Just show up on time; it's not my job to cover for you." That was my goal, show up on time. I worked for him less than a year; a new general manager came in and my boss was out the door in a few weeks. Guess the new GM had higher goals than just showing up on time. The lobby bar crew was nervous about getting a new boss; I was looking forward to it. It certainly could not be worse, could it?

The new boss sent shock waves through the hotel. He came in on fire. The numbers were a mess, profit was way down, and costs were way up. In our first management meeting he was so agitated that he paced around the perimeter of the room while telling us what a horrible job we were doing. One of the drinking crew piped up that the old boss kept putting off writing policies and procedures. That was a big mistake. Our new boss pounded his fist on the table, making it clear that it was our fault; we knew what had to be done and we should have done it ourselves. I remember the executive chef cursing and storming out of the meeting. I tried to like our new boss. He was everything I had wanted, wasn't he? Totally hands on, jumped in whenever needed, always out on the restaurant floor, never in the lobby bar. Be careful what you wish for. He never saw anything positive in anything. New policies and procedures were dropped in your employee mailbox, literally a physical mailbox; this was before email. Communication was yelling when things did not go well and saying nothing after a job well done. He judged us by the mess our old boss had left; he was ready to clean house and you could sense we were all in the way. He never bothered to ask us how we felt about the operation; he assumed we were part of the problem. Our old boss did not want input because he was lazy; this guy did not want input because he thought he was brilliant.

It took me about two months to decide he was awful, and I was not alone. The entire staff started talking badly about him behind his back. It finally exploded when he unloaded on the sous chef in the middle of a dinner rush and the chef walked off the job. Others became empowered and went to Human Resources to complain; the result was an anonymous management survey. It seemed like a waste of time to me. Why not just have a meeting where everyone could talk freely, with HR and our boss present? All the biggest complainers were insistent on a survey. The results were not good; HR and upper management feared others would walk out so they sat down with us and reviewed the results. Once again, I raised my hand and said we need to have a face-to-face meeting. Let him explain why he was managing us with an iron fist.

A meeting was finally agreed upon. We all arrived in a banquet room; a large U-shaped table was set up for the 15 of us. HR was seated on the side of the room. We took our seats; he walked in and stood right in the center of the U-shaped table so he could tower over us. He stood the whole time and started the meeting by announcing that this was our chance to get any complaints off our chest. HR did nothing to facilitate a discussion. It was intimidating. No one said a word and you could see a smirk forming on his face. I decided I was not leaving without saying how I felt. I did not hold back. After I finished, one of the banquet managers piped in with a few lame complaints. All the big talkers sat there paralyzed with fear. I looked around that room at managers who had wasted hours of my time complaining about this guy. Now they were silent, looking down at their hands trying to be invisible. I pledged to never put myself in such an embarrassing situation with a boss again. If I had issues, I would deal with them privately and not get caught up with the mob. Within weeks, managers and chefs started to leave the hotel; most quit and went to work for different hotel chains. Our boss was never able to show any humility after the meeting. He took the whole process personally and refused to acknowledge his role. After the meeting he pretended that I did not exist. But he had met his match with me. I was not going to leave; I had avoided most of his wrath because my restaurant was running so well. I learned so much watching how poorly he handled his team and how easily it imploded — mistakes I would try hard never to repeat. He went on to hop from company to company. My guess is he never found humility.

Managing with a strong personality takes a lot of finesse. As a woman I learned quickly that my intense personality was going to rub a lot of people the wrong way. At work I have been screamed at, cussed at, and even had a chef throw a knife in my direction. But I was not going to get away with losing my temper like the men with whom I worked. Unfortunately, when there is a line of customers at the door, the kitchen is backed up and the chef is screaming, it is easy to add fuel to the fire by raising your voice at your staff. Your employees are constantly judging you by how you present yourself. You must give your team many opportunities to be open with you on the little things, so when big things happen, they do not feel intimidated to approach you. You can never make excuses for your behavior. The day that the chef walked out, our boss should have been the one to call the meeting, not HR. He should have acknowledged his temper because we all saw it. It would have been the perfect time to hit restart with our support but instead he alienated us more. Just because your badge says boss does not mean you do not need the support of every member of your team. Ultimately you will fail without it, and he did.

Jealousy and envy in the workplace are a fact of life. The success of others is not always celebrated, and sometimes people are in jobs for which they do not have the skills. We do our young employees a huge disservice by not mentoring them to anticipate the myriad of emotions and experiences they will encounter. They are going to have disappointments in life and many of those disappointments are going to be in the workplace. I have been passed over and looked over. I have been envious of others and wished failure on a boss (more than once). Some of my worst management mistakes were with females. I wish I had been afforded more opportunity, especially as a young manager, to work with and for women. It took many years and many mistakes before I learned to work effectively with women in management above and below my position.

I can share one of the worst examples. I was promoted to food and beverage director, the first female to ever have the job in this particular hotel. The same day I was promoted they announced a new woman hired from outside the hotel to fill my former position as catering director. They did not include me in the hiring process even though she would report directly to me. They had allowed the outgoing male food and beverage director to hire one of my key team members. She had zero hospitality experience but as soon as I met her I knew why he had hired her. She was young, very attractive and dressed beautifully. We were oil and vinegar. I started judging everything she did and comparing it to how I would have done it. I was embarrassed that my male bosses did not trust me enough to let me hire my own (experienced) catering director and my entire staff knew it. I took out my irritation on her and gave her zero guidance — so much for being a mentor. I was cutting off my nose to spite myself because I wanted her to fail.

My boss, the general manager of the hotel, was an older gentleman with gray hair, in his late 60s. He and I had a very supportive relationship. The struggle between my manager and me was too much for him to handle. I put him in an awful position by taking advantage of our years of working together and constantly complaining about her. Finally, the three of us sat down to air our differences. He had not set expectations for the meeting; he just wanted the problem to go away. The meeting only made things worse. He treated us differently because we were women. He talked to us kindly, but as if he was our dad scolding us for bad behavior. In retrospect, he set us up for failure by not setting his expectations for the meeting. We should have each had a chance to talk about our issues. Then he should have shifted the conversation to his expectations. We each should have been asked what we were willing to do to ensure the success of the department. We were causing stress to each other and to the people who worked for us. I knew better; I was more to blame because I was her boss.

Two days later my boss came into my office and announced that HR was hiring a professional counselor to help us resolve our problems. He referred to us as 'you girls.' We were both in our 30s; I was mortified and honestly baffled. There were many men that I worked with in my career that did not work well with each other, especially the chefs. They fought and screamed at each other. No one had ever been sent to counseling. This was not a girl problem; it was two professionals being envious of each other. I refused to give her the guidance and training she deserved and when I finally offered it, she would not accept it. No counselor could fix our issues; it was up to me. I asked her to meet me off property for lunch one day. I led with a statement that if we could not work this out, one of us was going to end up losing her job. I assured her we were both at risk. I explained that I resented the way she was hired; I wanted her to understand my misplaced anger. Then I told her I would do whatever I could to fix our professional relationship. We did not need to like each other, but we needed to be successful together. I had foolishly refused to see the part I played until it was too late. I had discounted her from day one because she was someone else's choice; not mine. We both could have been so successful if I had taken a different approach. There was no happy ending. She and I worked together for a few more months. I am guessing she started looking for a new job the day after our lunch.

I was her boss and I had failed her. I did not end up in a conference room with a bunch of unhappy managers, but it took time to mend the damage. I had pushed her out and everyone saw it happen. She was not given the same level of communication and mentoring I prided myself in giving my team members. It taught me that if you want to be a leader, mentoring is an obligation, not a choice. Being the boss comes with responsibilities. I missed an incredible opportunity to reach out and pull up another woman because I let my ego get the best of me. As for my boss, he was just happy he did not have to deal with the strife anymore. It was not his finest hour either.

Changing Course

As it turned out, a career in the hospitality industry was better suited for young single people. Marriage and parenting suffer when you work long unpredictable hours. Looking back, my bosses were all men; most did not have families. The few that did were ambitious and on the fast track to be hotel general managers. If I had gotten to a higher level before I had my first child, I could have balanced my family life with job responsibilities better, but I did not get there fast enough. I should have. I am realistic looking back as a much wiser woman; what held me back was my determination to be true to myself in a world of men. Maybe I was foolish; it did cost me time on my career trajectory. But now as a much more seasoned woman manager, it was worth it. If I had played the game better, I would have missed many life lessons that stick with me today.

In the 1980s and 1990s things were much different for women in the workplace, especially women in upper management. There were very few of us and maternity leave was usually six weeks, unpaid. If you were lucky, you would come back to the job you had when you left but there was no guarantee. Those six weeks could set your career back a year. There is a price to be paid for having it all. I know women feel that they have the right to have it all, but in the context of a family, you must make sure that the welfare of your children is covered first. It was important that my husband and I were on the same page about what our priorities were. We agreed that raising our children was both our responsibilities.

I never wanted to be a stay-at-home mom like my mother. That conversation is much more than words; you must be aligned philosophically. Once you start having children, control is lost. Life moves forward whether you are in the boat or hanging on for dear life. Leadership skills are out the window. The kids sure do not care about your resume. I went from confident and in charge to hair on fire. My husband did not fare much better, and together we were like the inside of an old golf ball filled with hundreds of layers of rubber bands, unwinding and popping until years later when the core would be exposed. When you are young and daydream about having a family, you picture yourself with perfect children. Mine were not. My daughter was born with an opinion (the opposite of mine); my son only slept when I was awake. Career and motherhood are so difficult for women to balance. I see women all the time, trying to keep up with men in the workplace. You are fooling yourself. We have a force in us that is so strong. Motherhood is powerful. We make the best decisions we can, but the guilt is always there.

The move from Alaska to Virginia seemed the perfect time to take a real break from my career and my guilt. I had watched the fulltime moms in our squadron family for years; they loved being home with their children and I had always wondered if I was missing out. My husband's new staff job was 8 to 5 with little travel. It would be the perfect opportunity to spend more time together as a family. I knew I could go back to work if we needed the money but if I was going to try fulltime motherhood, this was my chance.

In my mind everything was planned out. I had considered every possibility except the one that would happen. Saying goodbye to Alaska was saying goodbye to the career that had filled my soul for 14 years. It was who I was, what I did best, the job where everything made sense. If I had known that leaving Alaska would be the end of my hospitality career, I am not sure I would ever have left. To this day I sit down at a restaurant table and rearrange the silverware. I miss the energy; I miss the daily detail to service. I am grateful to this day that I walked into that Anchorage hotel; the memories I made there would have to last a lifetime.

I have always been guilty of planning too much and not living enough. We found a house in Yorktown, Virginia, in a lovely, master-planned community called Kiln Creek. Things were falling into place just like I had planned, or so I thought. My husband was no longer flying; he was filling a staff requirement. I was no longer working outside the home; I was a stay-at-home mom. We had never lived on one income, and even though we had planned for it financially, I had not realized how much my self-worth came from my paychecks. The transition affected parts of our life and marriage we never could have anticipated. The neighborhood was our life preserver as we both struggled to stay afloat in our new situation. I loved having neighborhood friendships, meeting the other moms every morning at the school bus, getting together for coffee and watching the kids play in the backyard, jumping rope, riding bikes, and catching fireflies during warm summer nights. We even had those potlucks we loved in the military. Pizzas or casseroles with a bottle of wine and great conversation, we enjoyed those gatherings. My daughter had friends in the neighborhood for the first time and even a best friend. There were sleepovers, birthday parties, and dozens of trips to Busch Gardens amusement park with friends. For years I had daydreamed about how my days would be filled if I only had the time. I had been envious of the military wives who always seemed to be doing something together. Now I was finally living my daydream.

Looking back now, those were tough years for our marriage. We had a great plan that did not work in our real lives. We took on more traditional roles and responsibilities for the first time. My husband brought home the paycheck and I managed the home. It sounded good but we had not anticipated the impact two major job changes at the same time would have on our relationship. I was always some degree of exhaustion from children, groceries, cooking, laundry, and housework. It was a new dynamic. I thought I could manage my children like I did my management team, but the two kids and the dog were running the show. The lifestyle we had during the years before our second child was born allowed us both to be selfish. Hunting, fishing, working odd hours, we juggled it all perfectly. This new life was mundane compared to the exciting life we had left. Those years in Virginia became the beginning of the unraveling. Looking back, I do not see how it could have happened any differently.

Months after settling in, my 6-year-old daughter had a particularly stressful morning, ten times worse than her usual refusal to wear something besides her pajamas to school. She woke up mad at the world, refused to get dressed for school, and cried when she saw her breakfast (the same thing she loved the day before.) She missed the bus and threw a tantrum the entire drive to school. Once I got her into the hands of her teacher, she looked back at me and said she hated me and loved her teacher. Meanwhile, the baby decided he had enough and proceeded to screech at a piercing level the whole way home in the car. That morning it was too overwhelming; I walked in the house, put my son in his play swing and went to find my resume. When my husband got home that evening, I made an excuse to run to the store. Instead, I dropped my resume off at the local Omni hotel. I drove home feeling like I was a failure. I had planned for so long. I had what I thought I wanted, and I was not happy. When the hotel called me the next day, I did not answer the phone. I just let it go to the answering machine and never returned the call. I deleted it before my husband got home. I did not want to admit what I had done because I thought he would tell me I should go back to work if I was unhappy. If I was offered a job, I did not think I would be able to say no. We had planned for the financial hit but not the hit to my self-esteem. It was the first time since babysitting as a preteen that I did not have my own money. I felt selfish because I wanted it all.

I was brought up in a house where my mother was home all the time and my parents had made it work. However, I could not come to terms with getting a great education, working so hard to build a career, and then just giving it all up. Moving back east was never going to be anything other than figuring out how to survive all the changes we chose. All the planning in the world was not going to make things magically work. My husband missed flying; we missed the squadron community. I missed my hotel colleagues. They were moving on with their careers, still chasing promotions. I was not a player anymore. We were no longer getting the energy outlet our jobs had provided. My husband needed the adrenaline that came from flying. He needed the camaraderie being around the guys in the squadron. I needed to be the boss; I missed managing a team, constantly answering questions, solving problems, meeting with clients, being at the center of social events. Doubts about what was next were starting to creep in as we got closer to 15 years in the military. Would there be a promotion to a higher rank, or would it be early retirement? Knowing huge decisions were ahead added to our stress.

It was time to change how I was looking at things. What I had learned in business about getting out in the community and making connections could work whether I had a paying job or not. Leaving my career and moving across the country was like someone turning off the spigot when you are dying of thirst. The professional loss was difficult, but the hit to my confidence as a woman was worse. Did I just need to accept that I would not feel that same fulfillment doing simple day in and day out things? No. I loved being a mom, being close to family, having great neighborhood friendships. I needed to find something else to fill the gap that fit in with our new normal.

I challenged myself to be a success in my family life like I was in my career. I channeled my energy into new hobbies, planning activities for my children, swimming lessons for our son and beginner golf for our daughter. I planned neighborhood events and creative birthday parties. I even sewed my children's Halloween costumes (before Pinterest) and helped organize a neighborhood Halloween parade. I bought a bread maker and immersed myself in freshly baked bread of every imaginable type, always bringing a loaf or two to every get together. I found a woman who could watch my son for a few hours twice a week so I could take painting lessons at the local Recreation

Center. I picked up my golf clubs again and joined a women's golf group. I started making connections again. The connections did not look the same; they were hobby related not career related, but it filled my need for learning and meeting new people. I even volunteered to work the polls during local elections. One of our neighbors ran for the local Board of Supervisors and I jumped in to volunteer on her campaign. I was no longer planning events for local politicians, but I certainly could volunteer for them.

I learned the value of slowing down, owning my own happiness, and just enjoying where I was in my life rather than struggling over what-ifs. I started to look forward to mornings at the bus stop and afternoon chatter before the bus arrived home. There was joy watching my daughter run from one house to the other playing with friends. Now I look back with much wiser eyes. It was a wonderful time for our children, and we made incredible friends. I wish I had realized earlier that happiness would not come automatically; I would have to fight for it just like I had in my career.

Previously being driven to have a certain lifestyle that included intensity at every level, now thinking that I could handle the opposite was naive. I contributed to the unhappiness growing in our marriage. We had both agreed that I would stay home with our children, yet I was the one feeling cheated, that I had given up more. Self-pity is a dangerous thing. The struggle in our marriage had moved in and taken a seat at our table. Time was moving on, and we were getting closer to deciding about our future in the military. I started to feel hopeful that there would be a chance to reset. I learned so many times as a young child that moving meant starting over again. Maybe this time it would be a positive thing; we certainly needed it. In a year our son would be ready for a preschool program. Then maybe we could look at things differently and be happier together. All the lessons learned, the years invested, the good and the bad might just be because there is a bigger opportunity out there. Nothing you could have ever anticipated but being ready makes all the difference. Deciding what to do next was taken out of our hands by a visit from my dad.

WHEN THE TIMING IS RIGHT

In 1985 I was single and working in Rochester, New York, when my dad called me to tell me he had done the one thing I never imagined — he 'quit.' Well, that was how I took it. He was 54 and had worked for the same company since his college graduation, climbing the corporate ladder for three decades, my whole life. To me, it was his identity; in some ways it was mine. My parents exemplified the American dream; I was proud of everything they had accomplished. So many moves, new cities, houses, and schools. How many tears had I cried? How many times was I told it was for a better future? I was a bit stung. My childhood had been uprooted over and over. Now, out of nowhere, my dad was walking away from everything he had worked for to start his own company. I thought he was crazy. Why give up a sure thing? The paycheck? The title? The nice office? Why take such a big risk so late in life? My cautious dad was a sure thing kind of guy and R.H. Donnelley was a sure thing.

My father had never said anything, but the truth was, he was never happy being a corporate guy. He enjoyed the people with whom he worked and the customers. But what pushed him was his sense of responsibility to provide a good life for our family, to put three kids through college, pay bills on time, and save for the future. He was driven by his grandfather's dream, that he would be the one to go to college, succeed and change the course for generations of our family to come.

While I was shocked at his 'overnight' decision, I found out much later that Dad had been methodically planning for years. The idea first crept in and took hold when Donnelley sent him on a special, months-long assignment to work with the Belo Corporation in Texas in the late 70s. Belo had acquired a company that also operated rural telephone directories. The directory business was new to them, so Dad was brought in to review the operation, put people in place to manage it, and make recommendations for moving forward. He drove with their sales reps, made sales calls, and met small Texas business owners. He listened to their stories and learned how business was done in Texas. His eyes were opened to the vast business opportunity in Texas. When the assignment was over, Belo offered him a permanent position managing their telephone directory division and the opportunity to own a small piece of it. My dad could not make the move. He felt it would be disloyal to Donnelley and a financial risk he was not ready to take. He still had kids in college. The time was not right to gamble, but the opportunity he saw in Texas would stay in the back of his mind. He had never imagined owning his own business, but that experience gave him confidence. When the timing was right, he would be ready.

Years later Donnelley would make the decision to expand to the west and my dad would be tapped again. He travelled throughout Texas and California getting to know mom and pop directory publishers, learning about their operations, putting together deal after deal, and purchasing dozens of small rural directory companies for Donnelley. He loved their entrepreneurial spirit. They were mavericks willing to take on the big utility companies. They had found a niche market, producing independent telephone directories in markets where the utility phone service providers were the only game in town. Independents could sell yellow page ads at a fraction of the cost because they did not have the overhead; they were not phone companies. All over the country small publishers were popping up in large part due to two landmark decisions — the 1984 Ma Bell divestiture settlement and the 1991 Supreme Court case Feist Publications, Inc. v. Rural Telephone Service Co.

On January 1, 1984, Judge Harold Greene broke up the world's largest monopoly at the time, AT&T. The decision made it much easier for independent operators to compete. All over the country small publishers were filling a niche market. The big utility companies were required by law to produce a residential telephone directory in the markets where they sold phone service. The 'yellow pages' in each directory were just a marketing tool by which companies could sell enough advertising to cover the cost of producing a phone book for every residence and business in their service area. But it turned into a profit center and independents were capitalizing on the cream on top without any of the operational expenses of providing phone service.

In 1991 the Supreme Court ruled in the case of Feist Publications, Inc. v. Rural Telephone Service Company. Feist Publications was founded in 1977 by husband and wife, Tom and Roberta Feist. The family-owned independent telephone directory company published large area telephone books in Kansas. Rural Telephone Service Co.

was a certified public utility that provided telephone service to communities in Northwest Kansas. Feist purchased white page listings through licensing agreements with dozens of small phone companies. Rural refused to license their 4000 listings to Feist. Without the listings, the Feist directory would be viewed as incomplete by users and paying advertisers. So, they copied the listings from the Rural phonebook without permission. What they did not know was that Rural had purposely placed fake listings in its directory. When the new Feist directory was distributed, Rural sued for copyright infringement. In Feist v. Rural Telephone Service Co., the Supreme Court ruled that the white page listings in telephone books were not protected under copyright laws. Information alone without a minimum of original creativity cannot be protected by copyright. The ruling would pave the way for an explosion of independent publishers all over the country.

My dad and Tom Feist had become good friends in the 80s when my dad was purchasing small directory companies for Donnelley. Tom became a mentor when my dad decided to start his own directory business. Dad saw the opportunity for a smaller operator to put together contiguous county directories in rural parts of Texas; he soon expanded to Oklahoma and Arkansas. Word got around that he was fair and paid on time. Other small publishers who would not sell to the bigger companies sought out my dad. Sometimes they showed up with a shoe box full of customer contracts; sometimes there were not even contracts, just a ledger listing transactions. A few deals were made on the hood of his car in a restaurant parking lot. He tells the story of a small publisher from Arkansas who was in the middle of a divorce. His soon to be ex-wife said she would sign the divorce papers if he bought her a new Cadillac. He had been negotiating with my dad for several months but would not accept my dad's price. Dad remembers the call, "If you can be here tomorrow with a cashier's check, I'll agree to your price." Dad chuckles, "Everyone ended up happy."

The pressure he had felt for years to make sure all three of his children went to college was gone. By this time, we were out on our own. My parents took their life savings and became the first in our family to start a business. My dad had spent years developing relationships with the independent publishers in the Midwest; it was a completely different business model. Deals were made with handshakes. Your word was worth more than money. This was how my dad had always operated, and he saw how successful he could be doing business his way, one relationship at a time. Two key managers who had worked with my dad for 20 years helped him get his business up and running. They were good friends, trusted colleagues, and ace salesmen. Both men went on to build successful companies in Texas and remained my dad's dearest friends. The company grew fast and soon my dad came looking for help.

In 1995 my husband and I were struggling to accept the end of his military career. There would be no promotion to the next rank that year so he could continue at his current rank or retire. He wanted to retire. It was a depressing time, the end of so many things. My dad had planned to visit for our daughter's seventh birthday. He was driving from Texas so he could bring a Victorian doll house that he had made for her. I will never forget the day he was due to arrive. We had a big birthday party planned the next day. Our daughter had begged for a piñata. My dad was due to arrive early afternoon, so I took the kids to Kmart to buy penny candy to fill the piñata. While I was loading our cart, my daughter proceeded to start opening candy, announcing it was for her birthday so she could have some now. My 'NO' caused a great deal of crying and pouting. Of course, we got the stares; they did not even faze me anymore. I finished grabbing what I thought was enough and headed to the checkout.

When we got home, I noticed two little bulges in the back pocket of my daughter's jean skirt. Sure enough, she had taken two pieces of candy while I was not looking and walked out of the store. My gut reaction was to threaten to cancel her birthday party, but I knew I would not go through with that. Of course, I yelled and told her she could go to jail for stealing. Then I did something that hurt a great deal but to this day, I am grateful I did it. I went and got a piece of paper and hung a note on the front door, telling my dad that I had to run to Kmart because his granddaughter had stolen candy — we would be right back. This was before cellphones or code boxes on doors. I put the kids back in the car with my daughter screaming and crying and drove back to the store. She clutched my leg the whole way through the parking lot, begging me to stop and promising she would never do it again. When I got in the store, I felt all the stares as I asked for the manager. A nice young cashier told me the manager had left for the day, and I said, "My child stole from your store so I am sure you can find a manager for me." She winked and ran off bringing back a woman from the back office. The woman, in a very kind but serious voice, asked my daughter to stop crying. She then proceeded to warn her about stealing and what the store does to people who steal — police, jail. My daughter stared at the floor the whole time, tears rolling down her cheeks, then shook her head in understanding and quietly whispered, "Sorry." My dad arrived shortly after we got home from the ordeal, and he had a long talk with his granddaughter.

The weekend and the birthday were a success but eventually the conversation turned to what had really brought him to Virginia — the growing pains his business was facing. His two friends who had helped him get started and running had both gone on to start their own businesses, leaving a huge gap. They were his mentors, and he was theirs. My dad needed me. I laugh to this day and say it was 'oldest child guilt.' He knew I would not say no. I felt a strong sense of responsibility and obligation just like him. My sister lived in France; my brother was in the military. I was either all he had, or I was the one that he wanted. I do not know which, but he said he needed me to consider coming to work for the family business. I was realistic; I was unemployed and soon my husband would be too. We made the only decision we could.

Moving to Texas and joining my family's business was a big gamble, and I was nervous. I always thought my husband would fly commercially after the military, but he had no interest so we both needed jobs. I told my father that both of us would need to work for the company or we could not swing it; he agreed. I had never considered working for my dad. We had never spent a great deal of time together even though we always had a good relationship. Working together was a big step, not to mention I did not know a thing about publishing. I had my own career path but saying yes was saying goodbye to my dreams. Responsibility is a funny thing. I just shut my eyes and told myself it would all work out. I had not even asked my dad what he planned on paying me; I doubted he could afford me. I was right. It is hard discussing salary with your father, and I made the mistake of not negotiating up front. It was obvious my hospitality career was over. I would never run my own hotel. This time there was no going back unless I failed my dad. The decision was out of our hands. We had two young children, and there was no future in the military for us. I was willing to put our future in my dad's hands because I believed in him.

Consequently, we made one last move to the place I never wanted to live. I remember getting on the plane to fly home to California after our Texas wedding in 1986 and saying to my new husband, "Thank heavens we will never have to live here." Texas was too hot and too flat. Now there was a moving van in front of our house, and we were saying goodbye to the great friends we had made in Kiln Creek. I saw my 7-year-old daughter crying as she said goodbye to her best friend, and it brought back sad childhood memories. We would make one last move so our kids could have a forever home. It turned out to be the last move in more ways than I could have imagined.

THE FAMILY BUSINESS

My father had been in the independent telephone directory business my entire life. To me it was just my dad's job; I did not really understand anything about the industry. One day he had a beautiful corporate office and the next day he was running a business out of the dining room. My parents tried to sell their house, but Texas was in the middle of an economic downturn. A dozen homes were for sale in their neighborhood; they were just going to have to make it work. Three years later the business had grown enough to hire a couple of office employees in Texas and rent a small space near the Dallas/Fort Worth International Airport. He then started actively buying small directories in rural counties in Texas, Oklahoma, and Arkansas. By the time he approached me to join the business, he had doubled his office space and his staff. He had small sales teams in all three states with 14 directories. We arrived in Texas in late 1995; my husband joined the sales team, and I went to work in the office trying to figure out how much I did not know about publishing. What I did know was that I was the boss's daughter, and no one wanted me there. I spent the first two weeks shadowing each of the employees; some were not thrilled. You could cut the tension with a knife.

My dad made me aware that we were missing deadlines. Missed deadlines meant late directories which meant postponed billing. The mistakes were costing the company and threatening its continued growth. I figured out quickly that while I might not understand all the technical ins and outs, it was all about process. That had always been my strength. Once I started looking at how each step in the production process affected the next, I knew what to do. It was obvious people were missing deadlines, and no one was doing anything about it. There were no policies or procedures, but there were many excuses. By investing my time in trying to connect with each employee regardless of how uncomfortable it was, it became apparent that several employees were running the company their way, not my dad's way. My dad was out buying more directories, and his office staff was incapable of handling the workload. Their answer to everything was hire more employees. I decided to bide my time and play a bit dumb while I figured out how to deal with the mess. For a little more than a month I kept my mouth shut and watched and listened. I let the ring leaders assign me menial tasks like hours of mindless filing. I played along, but they were helping me develop my plan.

I might not have understood the business, but I understood my dad. He is a man of his word and assumes the same of others. Dad had put his faith and confidence in people that were betraying his trust. I did not inherit my dad's trusting nature. For the first month I waited until every employee went home at 5pm and then I would gather up their timecards and enter their hours on a spreadsheet tracking their clock-in and clock-out times. I watched people take long lunches or leave 30 minutes early or come in an hour late, and I entered it on my spreadsheet. When payroll processed their checks, they always had exactly 40 hours. They were clocking in and out for each other so that their timecards would reflect a full week. No surprise so much filing had piled up. Some of these folks had been with my dad since he started the company. I knew my dad would insist on giving them a second chance. I had been watching and listening, patiently gathering facts because I knew I would need to share everything eventually.

My dad suspected some of his employees were not giving him the straight story, but he did not know how bad it was. I remember the day I decided enough was enough. My dad had called a quick meeting to get an update on an important deadline. The head of the production department assured him everything was on schedule. I knew my dad needed to hear that, and he would be mentally budgeting what bills he could pay once the billing hit in two weeks. I knew her reassurances were fake so when I went back to my office, I quietly stood in my doorway and listened. She beelined it back to her desk and told the other artists in a panicked whisper, "Hey, I just told him the book was at the printer, so we need to get it started ASAP before he finds out." That was it for me, call it loyalty, betrayed trust, or daughter bear, but I came out of my office on fire. I became the boss that day and anyone who did not want to be on the team was gone within a few weeks. I told my dad what was going on and backed it up with facts. I never had to mention names; he told me to handle it and from that day forward I ran the office with his full support.

When I started terminating employees that had been with the company since day one, it rocked the office. There is never any easy way to let people go, even for serious cause. I pulled the rest of the staff together and asked my dad to sit in. The employees needed to see that dad and I were partners. I told them that we were moving on, moving forward with one goal — to be a great company, a company that reflected my father's ethics of delivering on what we promise to our customers. Twenty-seven years later those great employees in that core group are still working with us. They were the key to helping us turn an entire system around. Taking the time to watch and learn before speaking reflects on you as a leader. While firing employees is not comfortable, letting unresolved issues go unchecked poisons everyone. It was an opportunity to hit reset and acknowledge those that were doing their best and make sure they felt part of the team. It was time to lead.

Daughters want their dads to be proud of them. It is true for me to this day. That desire motivated me like I had never been motivated in the workplace before. I remember asking my dad what his definition of success for the company would be. There was so much on the line — our family's finances, of course, but really my dad's ego and pride. He threw out a revenue goal almost double where we were. I could tell he had thought about that goal for many years. Surpassing that number became my driving motivation. I had learned the value of being a mentor from my dad, using best demonstrated practices and fixing one thing a day. When I threatened to quit my hotel management job years before, this man expected me to never give up. I had taken his advice, and now he was my boss.

For my entire life my dad was a salesman; even when he became a manager and started climbing the corporate ladder, he was a salesman's manager. The only way I was going to earn the respect of the sales team he had put together was to make the production side of our business bullet proof. Salespeople always know your weak spot, and they are always aiming for it. I could only fix the production issues in the office with their help, but I could not earn their trust until we started hitting deadlines. Our sales team averaged 20 years in the field. I averaged zero. Everybody wanted to work for my dad, so he had been able to hire some of the best salesmen available. I knew what I was up against — experience, knowledge and cunning. I needed a pro on the production side to teach me all the tricks. Through my dad's connections we were able to track down a seasoned production manager on the east coast who had recently retired. My dad hired him to come to Texas for eight weeks and do nothing but train me. I needed to be able to do the job the way my dad wanted it done but I did not have 40 years to learn on the job; I had a few months and a team of great employees. The man was a game changer and became my mentor for many years. He was the perfect blend of mentor, connector, and motivator. Like my dad, he believed in fixing one thing every day. We developed production schedules, bid sheets, and sales canvas schedules that we still use today. He taught me how to get involvement from the sales team by educating and including them. There were no secrets in the production process anymore. If we were at risk of missing a deadline because of an issue in the field, we brought that sales team into the discussion. We made a smart investment in our company's future by hiring an expert to teach me. Always surround yourself with the most knowledgeable people and soak up what they are sharing.

It is important to recycle past lessons learned. Think through your past experiences and pull basics that can work in multiple situations. I just had to shift my processes from producing events to producing directories. Serving 500 filet mignons medium rare at 8:05pm is nothing more than a production process. Once we put it in relatable terms, I was able to draw comparisons to things that I had done in the past. I really was able to take off pretty darn quickly. I was a bit shocked and so was my dad. I had the drive; I just needed the knowledge.

I admit those first few months made me nervous. I had gone into dozens of hotel situations where serious problems needed to be fixed, but I had never taken those problems personally. When it is your company, you need to learn to focus on fixing the problem and not let the sense of betrayal get to you. It is more important to figure out how and why it was able to happen so that it will never happen again. We partnered with our employees by incentivizing them financially to develop streamlined processes and policies that saved the company time and money. When we interviewed potential new hires, we included our employees in the process. Each potential new hire would have a second 'observation interview' with an employee in the department for which they might be hired. The interview was 1 to 2 hours of shadowing. During that time our employee encouraged them to ask questions about the work environment. It was important that our current employees had a role in hiring future team members. We were rebuilding and growing and needed everyone's help.

Our lives moved fast those first four years in Texas. We finally sold our home back east, so we had the money to buy a lot and start building our Texas home. At almost the same time we were shocked to find out that I was pregnant. This time there was no planning. When our youngest son was born, there was no time off, we had a big deadline. Since I was breastfeeding, I would pack him up in his baby seat and head to the office. We set up a production line to meet our deadline, constantly communicating and jumping in wherever needed. In a family business you learn quickly that the company comes first. The buck stopped with me. Years earlier I had learned the value of pulling my weight and earning the respect of the team. As the daughter of the owner, expectations were higher for me, not just in the eyes of my dad but in the eyes of our employees. My husband was on the road all week, and I was in the office. It was not ideal, but I had the flexibility to drop my children at school every day and pick them up after school. My mom and dad were a big help. Our youngest came to work with me every day. The office was full of toys and play sets. I would hand him off to his grandpa when I had to be on a call. He had an office of built-in babysitters. Most afternoons after carpool we headed back to the office so I could finish up while the older two did homework. I even had a refrigerator stocked with after school snacks. Our normal looked a little different. For years my children got to see their grandpa almost every day. Some of my greatest memories are overhearing my dad in the next office telling his life stories to my children. As the kids got older there was much advice passed on from grandpa to grandchild.

When my dad got into the independent directory publishing business, he also became a mentor and advisor to other small publishers. He would spend hours on the phone helping new publishers navigate cash flow, distribution issues, and sales commission plans. He was never too proud to reach out to larger publishers and ask questions. He believed in copying best practices and embracing new ways to do things that had been proven to work. He also believed in giving back with his time and treasure by serving on the Board of Directors of the Association of Directory Publishers. Dad was a huge factor in bringing the Texas independent publishers into the national association. He went on to be elected Chairman of the Association and served multiple terms. In 2004 the industry awarded him their highest honor, the Wil Lewis lifetime achievement award. A decade later I would be elected Chairman of the same Association, the first woman in their 115-year history. It was one of the proudest moments for my mom and dad.

I made connections through the conventions and board meetings. I took the opportunity to visit other publishers around the country to learn how they were operating and what best practices we could copy. Over time I formed friendships with publishers who were willing to be particularly open about their challenges and willing to share successes. A small, trusted group started to meet periodically outside of the conventions. We shared sales programs, compensation plans and cost cutting initiatives. Over the years, as our industry changed and faced challenges, this group would become invaluable to me. To this day, we are honest and open with each other. We want to see each other succeed. Professional relationships are critical to your ability to lead in both good times and bad. Many times, when considering an issue, I have told my employees that I would check in with a fellow publisher and see how they are approaching it. It is important to have professional connections you can use; it makes you a smarter leader.

Our company was growing rapidly so we made the decision to build an office in our new hometown. It was exciting to be growing our family and putting down roots in the community. We had a team in the office and in the field that was committed to our success. My husband made the move from on the road salesman to in the office sales manager. With three kids, parenting alone during the week was becoming unmanageable even with all the flexibility and help from my parents. Too often dinner was fast food. We hoped this move would be positive for the company and our home life. When we moved into the new office, it was a huge celebration, a new beginning. We went from a rental property with wires hanging from the ceiling and makeshift cubicles in the hallway to a beautiful building designed by our employees. It was our way of thanking them and showing them how much we valued their loyalty and hard work. We hosted a huge office-warming party and brought all our sales reps in from the field. Everyone was so proud. The building represented all the hard work our employees had put into the company. Most of them had been part of the humble beginnings; this gorgeous building was my dad's way of saying thank you. That building would be our headquarters for the next 20 years.

Over the next few years, while the business was thriving, our marriage was dissolving. It was a mistake for my husband to join my father's business. My husband and I had never worked together and starting in a family business (my family) was not the place to figure out if it would work. We were responsible for different parts of the business which often had conflicts, sales verses production, and we could not separate those conflicts from our relationship. I think the fact that it was the wife's family that owned the business vs the husband's made it more difficult. It was my father's business, and I was his daughter and that caused a lot of tension and hard feelings. I was the one that wanted my husband off the road once the company was big enough to support a fulltime sales manager, but it was a mistake. My dad called the shots; I accepted that; my husband did not. That move put us on a path from which we could never recover. Every divorce is a very sad and private pain. After 17 years of marriage, three children and a dog, our hopes and dreams together ended.

GROWING AGAIN

Our time in Virginia taught me that I could get tremendous satisfaction raising my children while not working outside of the home. To do it I needed to be willing to invest extra effort, thought and planning. It was not always easy. Many times, I felt sorry for myself, but once I accepted that it was up to me, I started to embrace it. I took responsibility for my own happiness. Joining our family business ultimately gave me the best of both worlds. Would I have gone back to hospitality? Of course, it was my passion. Change means risk, and I am not a risk taker. It takes guts to start your own business. The stress of making payroll, paying vendors, taxes, and investing in capital purchases cause many stomach aches and sleepless nights. I understood that I was being given an incredible opportunity.

My parents made a decision that some could say was a roll of the dice. In the same circumstances, no way I would give up a 30-year executive position and put my life savings on the line. I have always been grateful for the opportunity I was given; it was huge. But I will not sell myself short; I brought hard-learned leadership skills to my family's business — fourteen years of being a team builder and a problem solver. I had been promoted nine times and transferred six times. I had reached beyond my position and into the community to build connections that benefitted my employers. I was confident that I could walk into any hotel and get hired in an executive management position. Women need to give themselves more credit for what they bring to the table. We must not shortchange ourselves. If we do not promote ourselves and our accomplishments, who will?

A few weeks after starting, I walked into my dad's office and handed him my resume, he glanced at it and said, "I don't need this," to which I replied, "Oh yes you do. I want you to see all my accomplishments; you are getting one heck of an employee." I do not know if he ever looked at it, but I did get his attention a year later when I received a call from my old employer. Turns out word had gotten around that I was living outside of Dallas. They were planning to open a new hotel close by and wanted to know if I was interested in a job. Also, they were paying much more!

Family businesses can be tricky. Work is taken home, and home is taken to work. Family gatherings turned to discussions about the office. Sometimes we got engrossed in a conversation to the exclusion of other family members. My mom had helped my dad in the beginning, but she stepped back from the day to day after the first few years. She had the option to work with my dad or take a pass. She took a pass. The company went through incredible growth from 1997 to 2012. My parents were able to travel and enjoy a lifestyle they had never previously had. I had never known my parents to go anywhere other than those weekends visiting battlefields and a company trip to Bermuda that my dad won in a sales contest. With my younger sister married and living in Paris, my mom was able to visit often which sparked the travel bug in her. Her 'later in life' discovery of travel inspired me to see more of the world — a love I passed on to my children.

It was exciting to be growing the business. The initial problems had been cleaned up; we had learned to manage our growing pains, and we empowered our employees to be problem solvers. Together we had become so much more streamlined, and we ran our business like an assembly line. Changing technology allowed us to be nimble and more efficient. Eventually we were running so efficiently that I was able to manage both the sales team and production. When we made the decision that I would oversee the sales team, my father's first comment was "Oh great, now she'll be able to argue with herself."

He was right because I had always had a tough time managing my expectations of everyone else. I am not proud of it now, but after the divorce I finally realized how much my own personality was exhausting me. I was a single mom and had three children and a business; divorce had given me much time for self-reflection. No one could live up to my expectations. If I could stop being so hard on myself and expecting things to always go perfectly, maybe I could moderate my interactions with others. In a small business there is nowhere to hide. Everyone had to deal with me, so it was a priority to make sure the work environment was not stressful, and if it was stressful because of my drive, I had to change. I still struggle with that today. I was tough on my kids (the oldest especially); I was tough on friends and tough on my employees. I think women often get caught up in thinking that if everything is perfect then they have it under control. How many times have we stressed over things that do not matter? How many times have we vacuumed the house rather than relaxed with family or spent time with a friend? Life is meant to be wrinkled, not perfectly pressed.

The new office building was not just a huge financial investment in the company but also in our employees. We wanted a place that was more like a home than an office. It was a special place complete with a model train room. My dad had always loved trains, so he had a huge train set built on a raised platform. It was HO scale; the most popular rail transport modelling scale using a 1.87 scale. Two trains wound their way through farmland, under mountains, along a lake and through a storybook town. There was a coal mine with real coal from the mines in West Virginia and a beach with sand from my brother's first tour in Afghanistan. Several of our vendors sent model factory buildings with their logos affixed on top. We even had a few company billboards along the road into town. Kids and adults played for hours, and it was a favorite of visitors to our office. My dad spent hours tinkering, painting, and building.

One of the things I inherited from my dad was the need to constantly have a project. My dad is always up to something. As he finishes one project, he is moving on to the next. Once the building was finished and we were all settled in, we both started looking for our 'what next.' Even at its largest, our company was a small-midsize business with 62 employees at our peak. As technology made huge advances, we were able to operate with fewer employees. The change happened over time which allowed us to take advantage of natural attrition. Dad and I were easily able to manage the company without levels of managers, which allowed employees to have meaningful input. When we had an issue in the office or in the field, we just pulled everyone together quickly to talk through problems.

I have never liked meetings. When I looked back on my hospitality career, it pained me how much time we wasted talking and not doing. We would go into meetings with long agendas that easily got sidetracked. As I became responsible for teams of managers, I moved away from mindless meetings and stuck to one-issue conversations. Sometimes it took less time and got better results to grab each manager and ask for their input, map a course of action and follow back up later. Having meetings for the sake of meetings risks becoming social not productive. When I came to work for my dad, I followed the same strategy. Once a week we would hold a 15-minute production meeting to make sure every department was on track. When we ran into an issue that needed immediate attention or input, we would call an impromptu gathering and give everyone the heads up on the one issue we needed to discuss. I would call them 'grab your chair' meetings where everyone rolls their chairs to a central area. We would knock out the issue and then roll back to our desks.

Every organization has systems and procedures that need to be regularly reevaluated. We get lazy when things are working well but you must constantly challenge yourself and your team to find a better way, sometimes even copying someone else's best practice. As we looked for ways to continue to improve our production process, we looked at one of our log jams — directory cover pictures. With over 40 unique covers annually, choosing a cover that made each community happy was a stressor. When we went with the local cheerleading squad, a parent was irate because her child was sick the day the picture was taken. Too much could go wrong and did. One of our employees presented the idea of highlighting student art in the communities we serviced. The idea blossomed into a program called

Art for Education. We sponsored art contests in the schools through local art teachers. Students turned in paintings and drawings that reflected their community. We selected the winning artist, and they received a cash gift toward their art education. Their school received a cash gift toward art supplies. Each directory showcased the winning student's art and their school on the cover. Our program, Art for Education, has awarded over $1.5 million to art students and their schools. We were streamlining our production by giving back. Our entire company could feel great about the investment we were making in the communities we served. There is always an opportunity, even for small or midsized companies, to support local charities or organizations in a way that promotes their business at the same time.

I still missed the constant energy of the hotel industry, and for several years I hated having a desk job. Looking back, it made sense why I excelled at it. I missed pouring coffee, setting tables, grabbing food orders. I liked being in the middle of the storm. There was always an issue or a client that needed my attention. I realized I was missing the physical exertion which is incredibly important to my personality. I can have a good day, or a bad day, easier than flipping a coin. I had to accept that office work came at a cost to my mood; I needed the energy release of a physical job. I needed to burn physical calories and release endorphins. Women must be tuned into their body. If you are going to be pulled a million different directions, you owe it to yourself to be at your best. I care more about how I feel than how I look because my hair has never gotten me in any trouble, but my mouth sure has. Women certainly deal with many other changes in our bodies and our minds, but there is much we can do to give ourselves a chance. Working for my dad meant working at a desk;

the worst choice imaginable for me. I needed exercise and I needed accountability. I had not set foot in a gym since my 20s when I got stuck with a Bally's membership that I could not get out of for two years. This time I would shop around, ask friends, and pick a spot so close to my office that I could walk if my car broke down. Yes, I was anticipating every possible excuse. For 15 years I have been committed, not obsessive, but enough to keep me normal. It has helped me to be more balanced in my approach, especially when things are stressful.

One of the biggest challenges for every business is hiring. When we rushed, we hired short term employees. When we took our time and were honest about the hard work, we hired employees who are still with us today. I realized when I was desperate to fill a gap or staff an expansion, I started skipping things in my interviews, especially for the sales team. The thing we have all become hesitant to talk about, especially when we are trying to hire, is hard work. Very few successful people got where they are without hard work. As employers we are often so desperate to hire people that we do not want to talk about how tough the job is going to be and the amount of time and effort necessary to be successful. Instead, we hire people who are unprepared the first-time things get tough. My goal was always to hire long-term team members, not short-term employees. I was realistic about our company when I was interviewing. There was no corporate ladder, no opportunity for promotion, but plenty of opportunity to learn and work for a company that valued its employees. We hired folks who fit; the ones that did not fit figured it out very quickly. Great sales hires were the toughest, but some of the best hires we ever made came from our own employees. We incentivized our staff with cash bonuses for recommendations that became successful team members. Sizeable bonus payouts were set up to coincide with the probationary period and one year anniversary of the new hire. Who better to bring you someone with great potential than an existing high achiever? When I was in the hospitality industry, I always tapped into the connections I had made in the local rotary group, professional women organizations, and chambers. When other professionals have a relationship with you, a common interest or cause, they are more apt to work their own connections to help you get the word out.

The company was settled and running well; the children and I had also settled into a comfortable schedule. I was fortunate to hire a young woman who helped me with my children, carpooling, after school activities, and homework. It gave our lives balance, and my children were getting to the age that coming to the office with mom was boring. Finally, after several years I was able to consider getting involved in my community. I wanted to have connections outside of my office. I wanted friendship with shared interests. We were here to stay, no more moving, and I wanted to invest in strong roots. As a business owner I did not have any peers at the office. Everyone worked for me. My only confidante was my dad. Many professional women find themselves in the same situation. When you are the boss, there is often no one in whom to confide, especially when the issues are company related. Balancing friendships in the workplace is especially difficult. Mentors are great and necessary but sometimes you just need a friend. I had learned many years earlier that office friendships have too many moving parts.

Before I was married, I was selected to work on an opening team for a new hotel in Rochester, New York. For three months, a small group of managers (all men and one woman, me) worked together

14 hours a day, 6 days a week. We spent every workday together, ate every meal together, talked shop together and quickly became close friends. On our day off we would pack a picnic basket, lawn chairs and a case of beer and head to Sodus Bay to waste the day away. We were all single, far away from our families and did not know a soul besides each other. After months of spending all our time together, everything changed overnight when a gorgeous young woman was hired as an assistant manager. She was obviously someone who had had a great deal of male attention in her life. The guys were immediately smitten. I could feel myself turning extremely negative toward her after just a week. She ruined our group of pals as the guys tripped over each other to get her attention. Yes, I was jealous. In my eyes she was too pretty to be any good at the job. I remember falling into a pattern that many women fall into when we judge women by harsher standards than we judge men. It was my male coworkers who were acting ridiculous, but I was judging her and dismissing her qualifications to do the job. I guess you cannot be gorgeous and competent! Friendships in the workplace can be tricky and I think it is a topic women should discuss more. I have always preferred the mentorship relationship because it is about learning, whereas friendship is about finding commonality. When you are young, the workplace can fill a gap when you do not have time or energy to build relationships outside of work. When you are older, it can fill a void at home. Either way, if a work friendship develops into a romantic relationship, be assured the woman's career will be negatively affected more than the man's will be.

Finding friendship and meaningful connections outside of work often takes time we do not have. To make it work, women must be very selective with how they spend their free time. Between career and family responsibilities, there is not much time left. Whatever extras you choose for yourself, make sure they fill up your heart and mind. Do not give time and treasure to things that do not give the same back to you. It is all on you to be selective. I have wasted too much time in groups that are not welcoming. I do not care if it is professional or social or even philanthropic. If they do not welcome me to their team, I move on. My time outside of work is as valuable as my time at the office. I also do not want to be around people who do not make me feel good. It is a simplistic statement, but I wish I had believed it decades ago. Women by nature do not want to ask too many questions because it might ruffle feathers. We like to show our agreeable side because we do not want to be called bitchy, difficult, or overbearing. We tend to do the same thing at work. We cannot be afraid to ask questions. So many successful women either do not feel comfortable reaching out for assistance or think it reflects poorly on them. I love standing in front of a group, discussing an issue, looking at the group and saying, "I need your help. I don't know the answer." It is acceptable to be vulnerable. We are not men; we handle situations differently and that can be powerful.

Women have the added consideration to be vigilant about what we put out there about our personal lives, especially when it reflects on your level of success or income. Whether it is the number of trips you take or the clothes that you wear, women are judged more harshly than men. The dress code in your office should also be the way you dress. Of course, as a manager, executive, or owner you want to dress with class, but work should not be a fashion show. How you dress and how you act sends a message to your colleagues and clients. Everyone today is judgmental, whether we like it or not, and in business, you need to consider that potential clients are watching. Do not make the mistake of sharing everything you do, everywhere you go, and everything you believe. People are making decisions that could affect your future based on what you are putting out there. Talk to women you trust; join professional organizations whose goals are for you to succeed. Surround yourself with strong women who are not afraid to give and accept kindness and honesty.

Doing Your Best and Being Okay with That

Women are hard on themselves and hard on each other. Is it possible to be a good mom while we are climbing the corporate ladder? I planned my pregnancies to coincide with our military transfers on purpose. I did it that way so I would not have to take maternity leave. My pregnancy was not the reason I was leaving; it was the military transfer. That seemed to be more admirable. I heard the jokes over the years when females would take maternity leave, and that was when all you got was a promise that you would have employment when you came back; no guarantee it would be in the same job. I had my eye on much bigger things, and I knew extended gaps in my resume due to raising children would be viewed negatively by a potential employer. In their eyes I was a military wife supporting her husband's career. For months before anyone at work knew I was pregnant, I had identified my replacement and was mentoring them to make sure they were not only my pick but also that of my boss. I gave my boss plenty of notice and successfully trained my replacement. I did not have to deal with maternity leave guilt. Never blindside your boss; have a plan when you know you are going to be moving on. Leave a job better than you found it. Ultimately, it is your reputation.

There is never a good time for a woman to take a leave from her job. It is always in the back of your mind that your boss is wondering how you are going to have time to do the job 100% when you have kids. What will your priority be, kids or job? It is rarely considered that your spouse would take responsibility too; rather it is assumed that the woman is the primary caregiver. Who wants to take a chance on women if we have taken extended time out of the workforce? The transition back into the workforce after extended time off is something many employers want to avoid. We are told all the time that we get to make decisions for ourselves; we assume that we will be welcomed with open arms when we decide to return to the workforce, but that is not always how it happens. To this day women are dealing with the unasked questions and unspoken presumptions every time they walk into an interview. How could we give up everything we had worked so hard for to stay home for one, two, three years or more? Will we do it again? Are we really committed? Are we done having children?

We must be open and honest with younger women coming up. It is unfair to tell them they can have it all. Of course, they should aim for it, but they need to be realistic about what they are up against. There will be tough decisions along the way. You have got to be honest with yourself and take a long, hard look at the position you hold in your company. Are you indispensable? We all like to think we are. That does not mean we stop fighting to make things better for the next generation of women, but when we mentor, it is our responsibility to be honest about how tough it was for us. The workforce has a long way to go. For those women who make it work and reach the top, they must use their positions to influence meaningful change for the women who have not made it and for those who do not have hope that they ever will. Women must do better for other women.

I chose an industry that, at the time, did not have confidence in the ability of women to balance management and motherhood. As women decide what career path is calling them, they need to consider the reality of balancing their personal goals and the requirements of the industry they choose. I went into my career viewing each promotion and transfer as a personal investment, one I did not want to walk away from just because I chose to get married and have children. I have met many women who still worry even after they have 'made it.' If you managed to hold on to your career through marriage, pregnancies, and maternity leave, you might be breathing a sigh of relief. But mothers know it does not end there. You always feel like you are one step away from losing it all. It is a constant juggling act between businesswoman and being a mother.

Once you get older, and your children are grown, there is much time for self-reflection. When it comes to motherhood, we judge ourselves harshly regardless of how great a career we have had. Was I a good mother? Could I have spent more time with my kids? Did I invest as much time in them as in my career? Did they suffer because I worked a great deal? Women are supercritical of themselves. I could have done things better; I could have done things differently. I wanted to have it all. Did my children suffer because of my ambition, divorce, dating, remarriage? I do not think many dads stress about those issues in the same way. I know we are living in the enlightenment of the 2020s when men are supposed to be in touch with their feminine side, but you cannot snap your fingers to change generations of family dynamics. Moms are still bearing the brunt of the judgment, especially from other women. Are we raising our daughters differently because of our own experiences? I was much harder on my daughter than I was on my sons. I have sat down with my daughter and talked about the inflated expectations I had for her. I heaped all my negative baggage on her.

There were moments in our relationship, especially in the horrible teens, of which I am not proud. She was spirited; I was stressed. We argued about rules, curfews, and choices. She was my first born and my only child for over five years. My personality was to manage her into doing things my way. Her personality was to do the opposite. As the oldest she was affected most by our deteriorating marriage. She was more aware of the problems and bore the brunt of her parents' disappointment in each other. High school is tough enough, but her father and I made it even tougher. I felt a great deal of guilt for my failed marriage and the stigma on our family and my kids. I did not want my daughter to ever experience that kind of failure. I tried to failure proof her by pushing her to excel. I wanted her to be financially successful so she would never be dependent on a man. I wanted her to be able to deal with any bad relationships from a position of equal power. I never wanted her to have to give up on anything because she did not think she was good enough, smart enough or did not have the financial wherewithal.

The end of a 17-year marriage, especially one that unraveled slowly over the years, is extremely painful. Our time capsule included college memories, starting careers, buying our first home, our first dog, becoming parents and having dreams for the future of our family. Intertwined monumental life moments were ripped apart. The ending of our marriage was sad, angry, and stressful; it was miserable. I had to make a conscious decision about how I would move forward. Could I move forward without being overwhelmed with so many uncontrollable emotions? For me the decision had to be made the same way I had made every decision in my adult life; it was up to me, and I had the power to choose.

The end of every marriage is different but acknowledging the reality allows you to take responsibility for how you move forward. You own you. The only thing I had complete power over was how I handled the unpredictable waves of feelings that often hit me without warning. It was awful; there were days I went into my bedroom, closed the door, then went into my bathroom, closed the door, and finally went into my closet, closed the door and screamed. I remember sitting in the parking lot of my office after everyone had left for the evening, turning up the radio and crying as loud and as long as I needed. Figuring out how to navigate those next few years was brutal, but each day I looked for a positive step forward, even if the only thing I could think of was that I was one day closer to being okay. I concentrated on doing the most important thing I needed to do — being the best mom I could be.

No one teaches you how to be a great single mom; I never considered I would fail at marriage. Me? No way. I was smart, responsible, attractive, and successful. We were not going to be 'that' family, until we were. I was embarrassed by my divorce and did not tell anyone besides my parents for eight months. I even hosted an event at my home and made the excuse that my husband was on an unexpected business trip. We lived in a family-centric community. Social media sites like Facebook were full of perfect family pictures — dinner groups, vacations, galas, sports events, mom and dad dressed in the beloved community colors. I felt bad for my children. I wanted to make sure my children never missed out on anything, so I pushed them to travel, participate in sports, do community service, and get good grades. I wanted to prove that being a single mom would not impact their lives negatively, so I worked harder and got involved in my community, all to set an example and look normal.

Now, years later, my daughter is a successful woman and wife. I see a young woman who is fierce, confident, and kind. She is more educated than I am and more talented. There was pressure put on her from both me and my father to go to law school. Each generation should accomplish more than the last; that was my dad's hope and, in many ways, how he judged his own success. My dad's expectations flowed easily from his children to his grandchildren. For me, her success meant I had not been a failure as a mom. It is an interesting dynamic between mothers and daughters because as I have been reflecting on my relationships with all my children, I can see how exaggerated my expectations for her were. She was my first child, and the idea that boys will be boys just rings in my ears because I do think on some level women make excuses for our sons that we do not make for our daughters.

One of the hardest things each of my three children and I dealt with was ADHD — attention deficit hyperactivity disorder and the anxiety and learning difficulties that come with it. My children were each affected to different degrees. Dyslexia was an incredibly humbling experience. My oldest son had been attending Montessori since kindergarten. We loved the school and he thrived there. In first grade his teachers started discussing his handwriting with me — maybe he needed more practice at home, even tracing was difficult. I blamed it on being left-handed. He and I both write with our left wrists curved inward. He was bright so he could cover up some of the struggles he was having as he began spelling and putting words together. I did not realize he was memorizing, not learning. In the second grade I could see the frustration growing as reading and writing assignments became tougher for him. I thought it was summer vacation that had caused the slip; certainly, he would get back into the swing. He did not. Eventually he started telling the teacher that he forgot his homework; it got lost or his mother accidently threw it in the trash. Fortunately, the school suspected what was going on and called me in for a conference. I remember the head of school saying, "Your son does not read or write at the same level as his classmates. We suspect he has dyslexia and recommend you get him tested as soon as possible." It was a kick in the gut. My lip started quivering, and tears began to well up as I fought to hold back the flood. I cried for days. I did not even know what dyslexia was. Was I a bad mom for not realizing he was falling so far behind? I admit he struggled with reading so most nights I would just read for him rather than watch him get frustrated, but I thought he was tired or distracted. I was good at making excuses when I was uncomfortable with what I saw. My son was suffering; he was becoming aware that he was not keeping up with his friends.

We had him tested and the results were clear; he had ADHD, dyslexia, and dysgraphia. Dyslexia is a language-based learning disorder. For my son he had difficulty with phonetics, sounding out the words and letters. Dysgraphia is impaired handwriting. We worked with the school and hired a talented tutor to come to the school to work with him several times a week. I watched VHS tapes on our old VCR (there was no YouTube back then) and read every book on dyslexia that I could find. In all my research pre-Google I discovered that one of the best schools in the country for students with learning differences, The Shelton School, was 30 minutes away (with traffic 40 minutes) from our home.

We were fortunate to find such a skilled tutor that my son adored; it allowed me a few years before we had to make the transition to the school in Dallas. I dreaded taking him out of the school he loved, the school that had been an incredible support, but it only went to the sixth grade and time was flying. I wanted him to have every possible opportunity to learn and to build confidence. I knew in my heart that The Shelton School in Dallas would be his best chance. The day I took him for his first visitation we were both nervous. He was anxious, worried I would not pick him up on time, worried he did not have the right amount of lunch money, worried no one would talk to him. We parked and walked up to the office to check him in. Before I could sign my name, two young students whisked him away. He looked back with huge, pleading eyes. I was there to pick him up 30 minutes early. He walked out of the school a different little boy than the one I had dropped off. He was smiling ear to ear, and I could feel my tears of happiness welling up. Every mother wants their child to feel they belong. I knew we had found the right place for him to thrive academically.

The most important thing he learned was to advocate for himself. It was empowering to watch. I had spent years constantly covering for him and allowing him to depend on me instead of himself. The new school put a stop to that. We chose not to medicate him. Shelton did not push it, and classes were structured in a way that helped him stay focused. I did not understand dyslexia, but it was powerful watching him learn to understand it, own it, and verbalize how he needed to learn in order to be successful; and he took me along. Dyslexia is like a very crooked road. You are going to get where you want to go but you will be taking a more adventurous route.

Socially it was hard living so far away from school friends. A last-minute movie or pizza was impossible. No matter how last minute, if I could get him there, I would. I never said no, because I knew how important it was for him to have a social life but often it was too last minute. Sometimes his friends did not bother to call; they knew he could not come. As time passes and after not being available too many times, they stop calling, and you start to grow apart. It was an emotional rollercoaster.

Their dad had academic problems in school from an early age. In grade school he had been placed in special classes. Back in the 1960s and 1970s no one really understood learning differences. He grew up thinking he just was not smart enough. He was very smart and would go on to fly jets; he was just dyslexic. When I met their dad in college, I remember doing English papers for him. He really struggled until I got ahold of his homework. Now I was recalling that as I drove our youngest son to The Shelton School to be tested. Dyslexia is hereditary, passed through the father; the chances were not in our favor. By this time, I understood ADHD and dyslexia better. It was so important to get our youngest tested as early as possible; we had unknowingly wasted time with his brother because we just did not know. The test results showed ADHD and mild dyslexia. We were able to schedule him immediately with the same tutor his older brother was seeing. Academically he was able to manage his dyslexia; he was an extremely organized child by nature and did not have dysgraphia like his older brother. He had excellent memorization and recall skills which helped him master reading. He mainstreamed into public school after six years at Montessori. It was smooth sailing until the first time he went through public school standardized testing. He was extremely stressed out about the two days of testing. He had always been a cautious child, hesitant the first time he did something new. The test totally overwhelmed him, and the results were not good. The school recommended, but did not require, extra tutoring after school. When he found out, he begged me not to make him go. I knew in my heart that the problem was test anxiety, not knowledge. I felt certain now that he had taken the test, he would be calm knowing what to expect. He aced it the next time.

The anxiety and worry would follow him. As he got older and started playing competitive golf, the anxiety targeted his confidence and his mental game. He did not enjoy competition when it counted. He loved being on the team, had an incredible work ethic, and was always a team leader, but he let anxiety fill him with self-doubt when it came time to step up in competition. His skill was often enough to carry him through, giving him an occasional taste of success, but often when he had a great round, the self-doubt would start to creep in and target the next round. His thoughts would start to wander. He worried more about what his coaches, parents and teammates would think if he did not live up to their expectations. You can never per-form to the best of your ability if you doubt your ability to play well when it counts. He was totally committed, worked with a great swing coach, a mental coach, hit the gym, ate healthy, practiced smart, and worked hard on his skills. His anxiety manifested itself in negative thoughts, and when he could not manage them, he could not live up to his potential. I give him credit, he never quit; through high school and college he was totally committed to golf. Sports also made things academically easier for him to dodge his learning differences. He was on a very regimented schedule in college, up early in the gym, classes, afternoon practice, study time, weekend travel, little free time. He had always been disciplined which helped him thrive academically. His first real academic wakeup call would be the same as that of his older sister, but he had the benefit of her wise counsel as he prepared for the Law School Admissions Test.

For my daughter, there were no unmanageable academic triggers during her K-12 years. Even the first two years of college showed no red flags. Things changed the summer between her sophomore and junior years. She spent part of her summer in Washington DC interning for our U.S. Congressman. She excelled, and the staff did not want her to leave. For the first time, away from campus life, she realized how many opportunities there were after college, including law school. She came home determined but stressed. She would have to hit the books harder than ever, and classes were getting tougher. When she graduated and took the LSAT, the anxiety became overwhelming. It was the first time she knew that the anxiety she had been barely managing for the last few years needed attention. She had seen her brothers' difficulties but never realized that her issues had some similarities. Her brother was attending The Shelton School in Dallas when she took the LSAT. As a young adult she could make the decision to seek professional help. We had her tested at Shelton just like her brothers. Like them she had ADHD. Her diagnosis was processing-speed weakness and reading weakness. Her performance results even note that she did not want to appear as if she was 'weak' or 'struggling' which added to her anxiety.

Looking back, she always had performance anxiety. She was stressed over other people's expectations of her, but I had no idea. I just thought she was high-strung and lacked confidence in her ability. I always considered it the awkward teen years, surely it would be okay once she got to college. She took on extra credit and excelled on special projects. If it was 'extra' it was fun, and she felt it fulfilled others' expectations of her. She reminds me about the semester in law school that she studied in Berlin. She stayed in every weekend while her friends went out exploring the city and taking a much-deserved break from their studies; she was on a deadline to get her writing done to make law review. I take responsibility for putting that expectation on her. I was so wrapped up in my dreams for her that I never considered she deserved to manage her own time and set her own goals.

Today as a young woman she looks back on the pressure her dad and I put on her growing up before the divorce. She was the oldest by several years, so she was expected to be the responsible big sister and set an example. With moving to Texas came the added pressure of being under the watchful eye of her grandparents, my mom and dad. We all seemed to be full of expectations. Later, after her dad and I divorced, there was even more responsibility and pressure as the oldest. My dad was proud of his grandchildren but also clear that they were expected to be their best because they had been given so much. When her dad was not really part of her life, her grandfather's approval became very important, but his style is not to be overly complimentary. He responds to achievement with 'good, you should be doing well' versus 'good, I'm so proud you're doing so well.'

I learned many tough lessons in my career, but none as tough as those I learned being a mother. I think the best gift you can give to your children as they become young adults is to have meaningful conversations with them about their experiences growing up — conversations that are full of honesty and teachable moments. Do not be afraid to discuss the difficult times. I am incredibly proud of the young adults my children have become. They are such better versions of me and their father; they took the best from each of us and added their own style, and all we really did was lay a foundation. I wish I had understood that sooner.

My older son was affected the most by his learning differences, and his struggles have always hurt my heart. High school and the teen years are tough. I wish he had had a more normal social life, but it was not possible. College was his chance to form lifetime friendships — friends he still travels the world with today. He has travelled and worked all over the world. He has spent months off the grid in the Norwegian fjords and backpacking through Southeast Asia, taken survival courses in the mountains of Utah, and lived in New Zealand and Tasmania. It makes me realize how important each child's own journey is. Learning does not only happen in a classroom. It happens as each person experiences the world. I know how fulfilled my son is now, but it is still difficult to have those conversations and to share with him the guilt that I felt and give him the opportunity to express himself to me. Fortunately, we have found a way to laugh about many of the mistakes I made trying to organize his life and do things for him instead of letting him figure it out himself. He tells a funny story about his college roommate freshman year which sums up how overinvolved I was. He recalls that he and his roommate could not have been more different. My son was a night owl, studied just enough, messy, and loved to have friends around. His roommate was up at dawn, a neat nick, studied day and night, spent hours alone in the dorm room. He always told me that he could not figure out how he ended up paired with someone so completely opposite. One day when we were laughing about the big to-do there was getting his college applications filled out, he realized that I was the one who filled out his roommate questionnaire. Mystery solved. I picked someone for him who would have been my ideal roommate; certainly not his.

Women feel the weight on their shoulders when their children are not thriving. There were times I would look in the mirror and say, "Okay, why isn't this going better? I'm one of the lucky ones. Yes, I'm a single mom, but I'm in a position that I can do the best for my children. I can afford the help they need. I have a great job and family support. I shouldn't be struggling like this." It is hard for a mother to say I have done all I can because we never feel like we have done enough. It was not always pretty but we did the best we could.

WHEN ONE DOOR CLOSES — ANOTHER OPENS

Kids, dog, family, business, volunteering. How could I be so busy, but so lonely? I was feeling sorry for myself during my first 'divorced' Christmas break. The children were at their dad's house, so I decided to sign up for Match.com. Dating sites were just starting to become mainstream but no one I knew had ever tried them. I had seen a commercial on TV which was aimed at lonely parents over the holidays. I was nervous but I talked myself into it by deciding I would only look. After a week of looking, I printed out the bios of two men I thought were my type. I needed a second opinion. My daughter, now a junior in high school, was not impressed. Together we started clicking through 'potential' dates. We did not agree on anyone, and I was losing my nerve. Eventually she clicked on a gray-haired, middle-aged man with a nice smile. She said, "This is the guy." I said, "He's not my type." His bio said he had a tattoo; my bio said no tattoos!! It took me a week and a dozen rewrites before I got the nerve to send him an email through the site; it took him longer to email back. We talked on the phone for a few weeks and finally planned a date. We would each drive and meet in a central place for sushi, each paying for our own dinner. I got my hair done and bought a new outfit; he cancelled. We agreed on a new date. This time I showed up in jeans and skipped the hairdresser. If it was meant to be, it was meant to be. He was standing in front of the restaurant waiting for me. I knew the minute I saw him; he was the one; he paid for dinner. His Match.com picture sits on my dresser. We married three years later. I am not sure how one person can change the direction of your life, but he changed everything. There was energy and laughter in our house. We were both close to 50 so there was no naiveté. Happiness opens so many doors and gives you confidence. I thought I was all those things, but I was not — until I met him.

When I met him, I met New Orleans. My first trip to New Orleans was to meet his family and see the city where he grew up. I felt a pull I had never felt before, a sense of belonging in this soulful place. After Hurricane Katrina devastated New Orleans in August 2005, we travelled back to the city for Thanksgiving. We spent two days driving through his old memories. A four-foot-high water line stained the side of his one-story childhood home, silently signaling that everything inside was destroyed. We drove out past his old neighborhood to the Southern Yacht Club where boats were still piled on top of each other like Pick Up Sticks. Everything was gray, sad, and beaten down. We drove out to his old high school, Holy Cross. We pulled into the parking lot, turned off the car and sat in silent tears. It would never come back. The once magnificent three-story red brick building was hollowed out, black holes replaced glass windows, wooden boards covered doorways. After almost 150 years, Katrina would be the end of Holy Cross in the Lower Ninth Ward.

Five years later, my oldest son would choose to go to college in New Orleans. I knew in my heart it was a sign. We bought a tiny 115-year-old Queen Anne cottage with Eastlake details. A quirky, imperfect jewel, bright yellow with four shades of blue fretwork and floors that creak. Decades earlier, the living room had been the neighborhood hair salon, if only the walls could talk. New Orleans, NOLA, is an old soul. The streets are lined with trees that defy gravity. Each has its own personality. The houses are ancient but happy like your favorite great aunt — stubborn, resilient, colorful, eccentric. New Orleans filled an unexpected hole in my heart, a place to get away, to find solitude, refresh, and recenter. I allowed myself to be open to the pull my heart was feeling. An unexpected door opened, and I am grateful I walked through it.

I had always dreamed of living in one place, making lifetime friends, becoming rooted in a community. I had my roots in Texas and my limbs in New Orleans. Texas and New Orleans were each half of my whole, and I was ready to move forward and try something new. My children were getting older; business was calm and consistent. I still missed the energy of my career in large hotels, all the activities, hundreds of employees; I never got that rush from our family business. We were methodical; data is quiet, but I am not quiet. I kept coming back to my love of government. I had watched mayors, congressmen, generals, and a Secretary of Defense move through events with ease, so confident, so respected. I watched them speak to hundreds of supporters, holding the room enraptured with their energy. Maybe someday I could move from the sidelines to the table.

My love of local politics had blossomed in Alaska, but I was always a watcher. I had never considered running for public office; we never stayed anywhere long enough. When we settled in Southlake, Texas, I continued to watch from the sidelines. Moving from the sidelines into the game seemed overwhelming. How to even start? Who are the people I needed to know? I made the decision to tackle it as I had every new job, every transfer. I made connections; I leveraged relationships and was a work horse behind the scenes. I used my management style to do what I had always done best, learn everything and become a connector. Women are hesitant to step into elected office because there is no hiding in the grocery store anymore, or at your kids' sports games, dinner parties or bunco with the girls. I had spent half my childhood wanting to be in the popular group. I loved my home, had a great business, was making friends and going to lunch. I was included. Politics was the last place I needed to be if I wanted to be liked. Who wants to lose friends (because I did), meet false friends (I did), or get used (I was)? In business you stand behind policy; in politics you stand in front.

When I was faced with the opportunity to run for the local city council, I wanted winning to be a sure thing. Of course, that was not going to be. So, I did what I knew how to do; I organized and solved the problem at hand with the help of the team, the connections I had made. This time it was not a promotion, or maybe it was my biggest of all. I left the house every day dressed to win, thanks to my mom who went through her closet lending me many tasteful suits. I tapped into the smartest and most strategic people in my community. I parlayed every relationship I had formed over the last couple of years into helping me win. I ran the way I would serve, the way I had managed for decades. I am tough, intense, and very opinionated. I own it! The women leaders I respect most own their style and capitalize on it.

When I won, it was very emotional for my mother and father. An affirmation of their hard work and sacrifice. My children were so proud. They had held my hand through tough times, and their love made me know I could do anything I dreamed. My husband 'to be' walked every step with me; he put me first and did everything to support me. It would build the foundation for our marriage. Because of my family's belief in me, I would eventually run for mayor and become the first female mayor in our city's history. I was sworn in by a female judge who would go on to give my daughter her oath as an attorney in the state of Texas. When I ran unopposed for my second term as mayor, my daughter would be the one to administer my oath of office. A moment of immense pride that I will never forget.

In 2015 when I became mayor, my community was like most — a long history of male mayors and an overwhelming majority of male elected officials and city staff leadership. I wanted to embrace being a mom in office in a city of families. I wanted to set an example for young girls and to take mentoring out of the business world and into the political world. I knew my strengths and knew I would be successful if I used them. I understood my unique skills; I developed them over two decades in the hospitality world and the family business, and now I was going to figure out a way to make them work in this new arena. I was nervous but my family's support was unwavering. They believed in me, so I chose to embrace my uniqueness and do it my way. Women have watched for years as the road to success is jammed with men; there is too much pressure on women to be like men. Many women think that is the easiest way forward, so they give away some of their uniqueness and make the significant mistake of trying to be like men in their professional lives. Surround yourself with quality friends and colleagues who are happy for your successes and supportive when you experience failures. Women are too quick to fault other women and hold them to higher standards than their male colleagues. I have experienced a decades-long friendship completely thrown away like it never existed. Be a woman who is willing to give the benefit of the doubt in friendship like you would to a male colleague in business.

Love your community and it will love you back. #IbelieveinSouthlake was my mayoral campaign slogan in 2015, and it became my message and the message of the city. To this day an 'I believe in Southlake' art wall stands in their Town Square for selfies. In late 2014, I was introduced to Jim Ferguson, famous for, "Beef, it's what's for dinner." I needed a campaign slogan that would tell the citizens what kind of mayor I would be. His process was simple but to the point. He asked me one question, "What do you love about your city?" Ten minutes after my going on and on about Southlake (maybe longer), he looked at me and said, "Sounds like you believe in Southlake." It took me a few seconds but then I smiled and said yes, "I believe in Southlake." I truly loved my community, and I was dedicated to celebrating it and inspiring others to love it too.

One of my favorite books is *Love Where You Live, Creating Emotionally Engaging Places,* by Peter Kageyama. The title states the goal: You want your employees to love their jobs; you want your citizens to love their community. I realized the greatest gift we can give our communities is engagement. Community involvement motivates others; it builds a community in which people believe. More often, we line up criticisms rather than compliments. We take from our communities without giving back. It reminds me of those freestanding libraries sprouting up in neighborhoods. You take a book; you donate a book. If there are more takers than givers, there will be empty shelves where a great community idea once stood. Your community should be like your favorite vacation spot. The place you return to year after year and pine for in between. I doubt you know about the local problems because you judge it by your own memories, the happy times and the favorite spots. The greatest gift we can give our community is that type of engagement.

As a leader in any setting, it is important to share little things about yourself that have nothing to do with the job. Looking for ways to make connections with large numbers of people can be done strategically but it needs to be honest. I connected with hundreds of my citizens over our shared love of dogs. Together we raised thousands of dollars and collected tons of supplies for our local shelter and helped get hundreds of dogs adopted. I used my platform (my voice) to promote something that was important to me and leveraged that to make a meaningful impact. My love of dogs turned into an opportunity for like-minded businesses to host events with me that promoted their company while raising money for our local shelter. One of our community's family-owned pet stores enjoyed 'Mayor for the Day' for their mascot Lexi, a gorgeous brown Labrador Retriever. Lexi joined my Rottweiler, Emma, at City Hall for pictures and a few dog treats. The community loved it, and it helped support a local business.

Everyone knows 12-year-old Emma; she spent six years hosting events at our dog park, community 'Walks with the Mayor' and she even made the cover of our local magazine promoting our dog friendly parks. She advertised our pet friendly restaurant patios and partnered with the city's 'Elf on a Shelf' for Christmas fun. She was joined over time by four donkeys. The birth of our baby donkey, LoLo, was a community event. Shared love of animals created connections that lasted because they were based on what we had in common.

Sometimes a connection happens quite by accident; sometimes you must do much soul searching or, in this case, sole searching. I spent the first seven months in office obsessed with being accessible. I walked in the Homecoming Parade and crowned the Homecoming Queen, decorated cookies with toddlers, spoke at elementary schools, attended dads and donuts, invited students to city hall to be mayor for the day, and sat on the stage for High School graduation. One dreary Texas December day something happened quite by accident. After 12 years of planning, the city opened their first Recreation Center, an exciting and exhausting all-day event, greeting families, giving tours, face painting, balloon animals, pictures, and hours on my feet. During the 3pm lull I found a quiet spot on the outdoor patio, right in front of the fire pit, and collapsed in a cozy chair with an oversized wicker ottoman. Dressed in jeans and a holiday plaid blouse, I had thrown on a cute pair of glittery flats. Thank heavens! My feet were aching, so I kicked back, feet up and closed my eyes to regroup. As I readied myself to put my smile back on, I took a second and snapped a shot of the inviting fire pit and hit post. The next morning, ready to post some pictures from the event, I clicked on Facebook and was surprised to see tons (an unusual amount) of activity on my page. Likes, comments and private messages. Huh? Was it the new Rec Center? No, it was my shoes. A cute pair of glittery flats; a pair of shoes everyone wanted. #TheMayorsShoes

I had accidentally found a fun way to connect through my love of shoes. The perfect shoe for every event. I could tell the citizens what was happening in town, what events I was attending, through my shoes. It took off because it was fun, genuine, and a bit self-deprecating. Yes, the Imelda Marcos jokes followed. But I am far from her, and I had hit on something totally genuine. I found the first of many ways to communicate with my citizens, quirky like me. Shoes became a foundation to build on; I would let people see a bit of me that they had not known before. What do shoes have to do with good communication? While posting pictures of shoes on social media might seem silly, it made a connection outside politics, outside budgets, taxes, and zoning changes. I let people see another side of me. I celebrated our town, our businesses, festivals, special occasions, and accomplishments through my shoes. If I was somewhere, celebrating our community, my shoes were part of the story. The high school art students held a competition to design a pair of community shoes. My shoes at an event were much more fun to interact with than a selfie. Everyone is some place doing something, and they are all posting about it. How do you differentiate yourself? It was not a marketing ploy; people are too smart to get sandbagged by a too well thought out plan. It just happened organically. It must be genuine, and it must be something you are committed to for the long term because it comes naturally.

In any leadership role, do not ever hand your messaging off to someone who is not as invested in your message as you are. Your voice must be recognized and always truthful. Little issues did not become big issues because people felt they knew me and could reach out to me for help rather than jump to social media to complain. Over the years the numbers grew, helping one person at a time. They would in turn share their experience with their friends. Eventually when folks would start a city complaint post on social media, someone other than me would quickly and nicely shut the thread down by saying, "Hey, have you asked the mayor? All you have to do is message her and she will get you an answer."

One of the best compliments a citizen ever gave me was saying, "I can't believe how gracious you are to people when they lash out in council meetings or on social media." Do I always feel like it? No, but I was committed to the long-term strategy. It is not fun having to take whatever someone in a bad mood is dishing out. I remember a man who always berated me on social media demanding I take a salary cut. It made me laugh because we were paid nothing; he did not know that and was not smart enough to just ask, but he looked silly because everyone else knew; we had educated them. That is why I think so few women choose to put their efforts towards public office. Women like to be liked. Believe me, it is not easy wheeling your cart through the grocery store and getting hammered by someone in front of the pickles. Once I became mayor, no place was off limits — the beauty parlor, grocery store and even working out at the gym.

When I was elected mayor, I jumped in with an Olympic level of energy aimed at outshining my male predecessors. I was determined to be the best mayor my city ever had. I was everywhere doing everything. I had a closet in my office full of clothes so I could be ready for anything. My first year as mayor was a whirlwind — ribbon cuttings, galas, meetings, luncheons, speeches. I lived in a blur until I realized it was not fun at all. I was spreading myself too thin.

I remember precisely the day I said, "This has to stop." It was a Friday, and I had overscheduled myself. My morning started with company meetings (for my paying job), meeting with a developer on city business, lunch with one of my councilmembers, video shoot for a local charity and then on to the airport for a 5:30pm flight to New Orleans. What could go wrong? After 7am at the gym, I stopped at the dry cleaners to pick up my suit for the video shoot. Perfect choice — navy blue blazer with white slacks. The video was important to me; the local philanthropy provides much needed support every year with food, housing and counseling for those in need. The video was to help them raise funds at their upcoming gala. Meetings done, lunch complete, phone calls made; I raced over to the shoot location, perfect time for a Texas downpour. I grabbed my suit still in the drycleaners plastic and ran in the rain, no umbrella. Halfway down the sidewalk I noticed the suit bag felt light. My pants were gone. Not only were they laying on a wet sidewalk, but there were two muddy shoeprints down the front of the pants. I had not even noticed that I ran over them when they slipped off the hanger. Hair on fire I ran in the door and right to the ladies' room to change. This video mattered to me, so I carefully positioned myself for the camera resting my hands over the shoeprints and did the job I wanted to do for them. No time to change so off to the airport, not worried about the odd looks I got at TSA. Lesson learned. The things you care about should receive your best.

My schedule was out of control, and it was my own doing. I needed to prioritize just like I had done in my career. This was no different. Saying yes to everything is saying yes to mediocrity and that was not the leader I wanted to be. I had forgotten to be a team builder, not a one-woman show. I had built strong professional relationships with the councilmembers who served with me; I had forgotten how important they were to my success. I needed to allow them to step into leadership by sharing the responsibilities and helping them build their own goodwill in the community. I needed to mentor them. They were my team and if we succeeded, the community benefitted. Each councilmember chose the organizations to which they felt a calling and those were the places in which they invested their time. We ended up being more places and accomplishing more, and no one was exhausted; we had a great deal of fun. Leaders deal with tough issues and controversy. Leadership is easier from the outside looking in. The judgers can always do it better, so how do you make sure there are fewer of them and more folks who are knowledgeable? You must create a process that is consistent. You must build a six-lane highway and bring your community along with you; they must see what you see and want to go where you want to take them. It is the same in business. You must create multiple ways to share information easily. So, what do you do in a city to empower citizens with the answers? Teach them the process, and the process must be clear, always followed, and communicated constantly.

The ability to refer residents back to our processes with the assurance that we would handle each development like every other development, and they would be updated every step of the way, helped the overwhelming number of citizens to step back, take a breath, knowing they could count on us as they always have. I believe there is no issue that can divide us unless we want to be divided or, even worse, our own citizens want to see us fail. You must accept that there are those people, and they will never change. Therefore, the process must be strong enough and fair enough to speak for you when you cannot. I had a friendly acquaintance, well, she is no longer a friend (imagine that), post that if I did not like the heat, I should not have run for office and maybe I should step down. Wow, nice, heaven forbid she would pick up the phone and discuss what was on her mind. You have my number, or maybe text me. Ironically, it was not even the issue at hand. She felt someone in her family had been slighted by the council. I understood she just wanted me to fail for her personal reasons, but I would not because the process was clear and had been communicated effectively and followed precisely.

There is nothing worse than having to take a controversial position and knowing that 50% (if you are lucky) are going to disagree with you. As a woman and a mom, I hated that my kids were exposed to the personal ugliness. How do you lead through the fog when people are not engaged? They certainly do not need to pay attention to what happens in their community, but they do not get to give themselves a pass on everything that has been happening before they started watching. Worse these days are the people who criticize their community with broad brush strokes while they have never participated. For them, nothing good or positive ever happened if they were not there, and they were not. I think much of it is to get followers and social media 'clout.' Where has personal responsibility gone, and how can we engage or communicate with people who have their own agenda? The only way is to go around them and their narrative.

Learning to clearly communicate these days is more the art of figuring out how to balance your way from one side of the balance beam to the other. It is mental gymnastics. Social media has become the old game of talking through tin cans connected by a string. Can you hear me? Yes, I can. What did I say???? Huh, no, that's not what I said. Communication in every leadership position is key. I have read so many articles on how to communicate effectively, use bullet points, keep it short, folks love lists verses paragraphs. I have miscalculated, and I have learned some humbling lessons. The meaning of your words is in the ear of the beholder. The danger is we are teaching leaders to be fearful of communicating in any meaningful way. If there is a communication vacuum, someone besides you will step in.

When things get controversial, people start Facebook pages. Some start them for the right reason — to open the lines of communication and unite behind a cause. Some do it because they are drama shoppers, never passing up an opportunity to create angst and mistrust. They take advantage of those that are not informed. Maybe it is to be relevant, in that warm and fuzzy Facebook way. The good news is their motives are transparent. Do not give them oxygen; go around them; have better and faster information. It is a game of cat and mouse. They need to appear to their minions as experts. No way, you beat them to every punch. You become the number one source, and most folks will happily shift away from the drama. Always be ready to fill the communication gap. Be a trusted source.

Some of the best advice I was ever given came from our State House Representative. I have used it in business and politics. I had been mayor for three months; it was August, our state was in serious drought conditions and in the middle of one of the hottest summers in decades. When city water bills came out, the citizens went into shock. Social media blew up. There was no way to keep up with all the complaints and demands. It was not going to end with an even hotter month predicted ahead. I reached out to a more experienced colleague, someone I had watched handle difficult issues, our State Representative, and I asked him what he would do if he were me. He told me to hit the issue head on, respond with my cell phone number, and ask every citizen with an issue to call me directly. The idea terrified me, but it worked. We let our citizens know that we were available to review their water bills; we set up a 'Meet the Mayor' at city hall and invited residents to bring their bills. Staff members from our water billing and maintenance departments were there, ready to help. The conversation completely changed when I showed I was sincere by sharing my cell phone number, but more importantly, we followed up immediately with each resident. Word began to travel. It also proved to be an amazing learning experience for residents who now understood their water usage much better and that meant future savings. Now they can track the usage on their cell phones, like tying the package with a bow. We not only communicated, but we provided customer care, education, and long-term value.

Making yourself available is critical to being a leader. Communication happens on multiple levels. It is not throwing a whole bunch of stuff at the wall and hoping something sticks. For an hour and a half each month, I held a casual event called 'Meet the Mayor' at a local business. It advertised the business and my accessibility. Citizens knew that one Thursday a month they could stop in a local business, grab a cookie, and ask me anything. They were well attended events with rarely any complaints raised, but if something popped up on social media, the first thing someone would jump on the thread and say is, "The mayor is always available, and she has a 'Meet the Mayor' event every month." We were able to immediately help people who stopped by with issues by having a staff member there. We also were able to draw potential new customers to the business that was hosting. It is a concept that can easily work in business too, being accessible in a casual setting stops a lot of problems before they start.

Everyone agrees great leaders need to be strong communicators, so how do you communicate value in an impatient world? You must communicate in multiple ways and in multiple places. Tap into your creative connections to help you think outside of the box. Always communicating the same way, even if it is thorough and accurate, becomes stale and people will start skimming or worse — scrolling on by. No matter the issue, people want to interact. Ask a question or request feedback; it can start a valuable conversation. The people that do not like you may never change their opinion regardless of what you say but speak with honesty, carry yourself with class and always take responsibility when something goes wrong. Leading a city is like leading any team. When you are the boss, you are a reflection of those with whom you serve and work.

EXPECTING MORE

Iknew from a very early age that I was different than many of the other kids. I had a huge personality with determination to match. I was born ready to manage everything I saw — who sat where at birthday parties, playground games, the Thanksgiving table. I loved being in charge. Of course, in grade school I ran into many problems with that kind of personality, especially with boys. They would call me bossy; I would call them babies. If I pushed them or hit them, they would hit me back. The teacher would send us to the principal's office. My parents were called. Right or wrong, I got a spanking when I got home.

I remember Robert F. Kennedy's assassination. Our teacher was crying when we came into class that morning in early June 1968. After we were all seated and the bell rang, she asked a little boy named Robbie to be class monitor while she went to find a television set so we could watch the news. I got up in front of the class and told Robbie to go sit down. It turned into a pushing match, which was no problem for me. Unfortunately, I decided the only way to win was to slug him, which I did and gave him a bloody nose. I was eleven. My teacher walked back into the classroom wheeling a TV on a tall wire cart; she took one look at me and Robbie's bloody face and burst into loud sobs. The whole class was paralyzed in horror; I was mortified. I was sent to the principal's office; Robbie was sent to the nurse. He was doted on the rest of the day; I was avoided. My teacher's words to me made a lasting impression. She said, "Today isn't about you. A man who was running to be the next president was assassinated and you couldn't be respectful for just one day." Dr. Martin Luther King had just been assassinated in April 1968. It was an emotionally raw time in our country. I had picked the wrong time to be a brat. She put me in my place in front of my peers and I deserved it. It is amazing that, as often as I was punished for bad behavior, my spirit never gave up. I have come to recognize that it was sheer determination. Determination was a part of me that nobody was going to change. It was up to me to learn how to manage it.

My parents were strict and never made excuses for my bad behavior. They believed it reflected badly on them and that was unacceptable in our house. I dreaded hearing them say how disappointed they were in me when I got in trouble at school. I learned to self-impose limitations on myself. Without strong parents I can see how easily children can grow up resentful of social etiquette or of not getting their way. They become adults who feel entitled to make demands or say whatever they want, no matter who they hurt.

Parents should be a child's first educator, teaching kindness, table manners, respect for people and property. It is so important for parents to set limitations and examples for their children. I respect my parents so much for valuing their role as my first teachers. I have watched over the last few decades as parents have willingly handed over much of their 'first educator' responsibility to their children's school. Moms joined the workforce and with both parents working, it became convenient to let schools take on more responsibility. For decades parents have silently endorsed the current system by their complicity. Now we find ourselves in a political debate in our public schools, and we act like we do not know how we got here.

Teachers used to call parents about problems; parents would take care of whatever the issue was. Then parents started defending their children at all costs. Stopping behavior when children are young gives them a chance to learn to self-regulate. Let them be disappointed, miss a birthday party or a sports game because they broke the rules. Let them learn when they are young. It is not about your popularity; it is about being your child's first (and most important) educator. I wince when I see a child in the grocery store grabbing stuff off the shelves, demanding that their parent buy it, and the parent responds with, "Please don't do that." Please? No! Don't touch that. It does not belong to you. Parents are too afraid that acknowledging the bad behavior reflects poorly on them. Not dealing with it feeds the beast.

I did not grow up travelling, eating out, or buying new clothes. I got one new outfit for the first day of school but if I wanted something more, I made it. My mom taught me how to sew in middle school and I was good at it. So good that she signed me up for Singer sewing lessons. Singer was the only name in sewing when I was young. My mom and I spent hours in the fabric store picking out patterns and fabrics. My babysitting money became my access to cool fashion. My sewing teacher said my work was so good that I should enter an outfit in the Singer World Stylemaker contest. I worked for weeks on my McCall's pattern, brown and beige hounds tooth double-knit pantsuit, painstakingly matching every seam. It won at the local level and went on to compete at nationals in Cincinnati where I received an honorable mention. For the first time my picture was in a newspaper, the Charleston Daily Mail. I loved the competition, the accolades and winning. My hard work had paid off and I liked the way it made me feel.

Had to share those seams!

Being in the local paper for doing something good got my attention. I liked being chosen by my teacher, I loved making my parents proud, and I loved the competition. I needed to find something that gave me the opportunity to compete consistently. I was not an athlete; I could not sing or play an instrument. My English teacher pulled me aside one day early in my sophomore year in high school. She was taking a group of students to a speech competition and wanted me to join the team. I was certainly good at talking so I did not hesitate to say yes. My mom had competed during high school in Catholic school competitions for extemporaneous speaking. She had told me all about taking the train by herself to Denver to compete back in the late 1940s. I jumped in with both feet. I went on to compete in poetry and prose reading and extemporaneous speaking on the state level. My high school history teacher saw my success and asked me to compete in the Voice of Democracy contest. I placed first in my high school competition, went on to compete against the winners from all 22 high schools in the region, and placed first. During my junior year I gave my speech, 'My Responsibility as a Citizen,' to dozens of community groups throughout our region. That same year I entered the American Legion High School State Oratorical contest. The topic was, 'What the constitution means to me.' My love of American history and the constitution opened many doors for me and helped me become a confident and effective public speaker.

The ability to communicate with confidence has been so important throughout my career but most importantly in public service, especially when I became a mayor. I was the leader of my community and my words communicated vision, positions on issues, and goals. We used communication to invigorate community engagement.

Communities have an incredible team of citizen talent; the key is tapping into it. It is the one place where everyone should be truly invested in solving problems together. It is where you chose to live, raise your family, educate your children, do business, and make friends. You should want your community to be the best it can be and to represent the best in the people like you who chose to live there. But that requires your contribution. Problem solving also requires being open to change, doing things differently and considering new ideas. It requires confidence in your team. It does not matter if you have seen the idea work somewhere else or thought of it yourself. Some of the greatest big ideas were just scaled up from small ideas, and some of the smallest great ideas were successful on a much larger scale. Whether you are a big corporation or a small mom and pop, in a small town or a big city, there is much to be learned and copied from each other's successes.

Communication also means being accessible. Most potential problems can be handled quickly if people know who to contact and how. These days there are so many ways to stay connected and to make yourself available. I would like to think that with so many ways to get problems resolved, the first choice would not be the one place were next to nothing gets solved — social media — but I would be wrong. Sometimes people do not really want answers. I know a woman who was always friendly in person and never hesitated to text me on my personal cell when she needed help or direction. She was not someone I considered a friend, maybe an acquaintance. When she had something negative to say about me, she would never reach out. She would post on Facebook group pages or on Nextdoor, pretending she did not know me and had no way of communicating with me. She was always passive aggressive with comments like, "Did you read what the mayor posted, maybe I'm taking it the wrong way, followed by her negative twist. What do you think she meant!?? Has someone asked her??" She did not mention she had my personal cell number and if she wanted the answer, she could have called. Luckily, she found my number again when she ran in to an issue with which she needed my help. Imagine that! Too many people need social media drama to fill the void of loneliness and to replace real friendships that are much harder to maintain.

I had learned a long time ago to manage my expectations of other people and not to worry about their reasons or motives. Of course, it stings a bit more when it is coming from someone to whom you are always available. But I had become adept at learning to manage my own disappointment over the years, whether it was being left out as a child, passed over in business, or snubbed by the living room ladies. It hurts, but when friends or acquaintances let you down, you cannot take it personally. Once you learn to manage personal disappointments, it becomes easier to manage bigger problems. Learning to compartmentalize prepared me for the stress that would come with being a business owner and eventually a mayor. When faced with a problem, I give it all my energy and attention. If I need to cry, I do. Then I make a mental list of who I need to talk to if I cannot handle the problem myself, and I come up with a game plan. I do not let it become personal and I do not start looking for blame. Both keep the problem stirred up. I never let my worries keep me up at night. If I cannot take constructive action, I go to sleep. Staying up all night worrying makes you tired and emotional. We solve problems faster and better when we are at our best.

Surround yourself with people that lift you up and do not let exhausting people creep into your circle. My circle of close friends is small, but they are my rock and bring balance to the larger group of casual friends and acquaintances in my life. Exhausting friends act like they want to be close but what they want is your constant time and attention. They want to be friends with you because of your position and connections. You need to listen to them and take their advice; that is the price of their friendship. Exhausting friends are constantly keeping score. They will exhaust you, discard you and then quickly move on to the next person because you have let them down. They have no loyalty to you but expect your complete allegiance. When I became the mayor, it was a public stage like no other I had ever experienced. The position attracted many people with opinions and projects. I reached out to valued friends, other mayors and business colleagues and asked them to be part of my team. First and foremost, my goal was to make my own decisions, but I wanted to be sure I surrounded myself with a safety net, with mentors. These mentors had wisdom, experience and wanted me to succeed. I valued their time and made sure to use their counsel to make the best decisions I could.

If you are going to ask people for their time, respect it. The value in connecting with other professionals is to grow relationships that are mutually respectful and that last. Unfortunately, not everyone in a position of leadership respects another leader's time. Some develop the bad habit of advice shopping. This is true in business and public service. We have all experienced the frustration of giving hours to a colleague who begged you to mentor them and connect them with others in your circle. You buy it, help them put together a plan of action, they walk away grateful and seemingly empowered, and then they completely flip. It turns out their style of decision making is to listen to the last person to whom they spoke. Like an exhausting friend, this person becomes an exhausting colleague who potential mentors start to dodge. Their weakness is an inability to stand up for anything or speak with conviction. Instead, they vacillate, telling each person they meet with how much they respect their advice. There is no helping a person like this. They may be in a leadership position, but that does not make them a leader.

I am very fortunate to have many loyal people in my life that have stuck with me. Becoming a public official while still running a business took so much of my time and energy. What was left had to go to my family first. There were days that I just did not have anything left for anybody else. I have talked to women who are in corporate positions, owners of successful companies large and small, and they say the same thing — their friendships suffer first. The true close friends waited and picked right back up where we had all left off. It has been interesting how many friends with whom I have reconnected, and they all say the same thing: We just wanted to stay out of your way, let you do your job; we could not imagine the kind of pressure that you were under, especially these last couple of years dealing with Covid. They are my loyal friends; the exhausting friends and colleagues are gone. They cleared out, I had nothing to offer them anymore. Yes, it hurt, some memories still do, but I have had to move on.

The first time I ran for public office was in 2004. I ran for a spot on our local city council. I ran because I felt I could make a difference in my community, and I wanted my children to be proud of their single mom. The next five times I ran to continue the programs and policies that were important to me. I had helped form dynamic groups over the years that had created wonderful programs and events in our city. Our city had so many successes to point to that I knew people would pick up the phone when I called and be receptive to partnering with us on shared causes. Over the years in politics, business, and philanthropy I had built a far-reaching group of connections. Together we could get big things done.

The most meaningful thing I took from business into public service was mentoring women, speaking about the importance of being comfortable with who they are and challenging them to be leaders, not followers. I naturally gravitated to mentoring young women as I could relate to their struggles. With community volunteers we started inclusive mother/son and mother/daughter service groups, SASO (Scholars and Athletes Serving Others), so moms and their teens could spend quality time together doing meaningful community service.

Partnering with community leaders, we started organizations that benefit children. Our city, school district and chamber joined forces to start SKIL — Southlake Kids Interested in Leadership. Our goal was to give high school juniors the opportunity to interact with elected officials, city staff and business leaders. The year-long program challenged the students to be part of meaningful change in our city by giving them a seat at the table. They learned to balance new ideas with process. They learned how to approach change by first understanding city ordinances and regulations and the importance of the taxpayers who pay for all city services. We connected the students with corporations in our city where they took on an issue posed by the company and presented their findings to the company's leadership. The goal of SKIL is to teach our future leaders that to make meaningful change you need to have a seat at the table.

Giving back is important but do not make the mistake of over committing. One of the things I have learned working on big projects is that there are people, mostly women, that suffer from an inability to say no. There are those who always raise their hand to help but rarely come through. They never had the time to say yes in the first place. If you do not have the time, energy, or passion, it is going to become obvious quickly. Saying no should be empowering because it shows you value your time and effort. I learned the art of saying no listening to my dad in the next office for 24 years. I knew when he liked a cause but did not want to serve on a working committee because he would give them my name and assure them that I would love to do it. He looked good and I did the work; we were a great team. It was a great benefit to me when I was new to Texas and trying to make connections. The people calling him would never have even known I existed. I made incredible, long-lasting connections and had the opportunity to serve on boards for philanthropic organizations that did meaningful work, serving those in need in our community. Over the years, those causes, and charities became important in making me the kind of leader I would be in public office.

Leaving elected office after almost 14 years was extremely emotional for me. Being mayor was being part of the greatest team I had ever experienced. I relished the pressure. I was motivated by the issues, the problem solving, connecting people to get things done, the cheerleading for my community, and working with the amazing staff and volunteers to make my city an incredible place to live. I did my best, leading with honesty and integrity. Hard work and determination pay off. Isn't that the goal? I was leaving with no regrets and a legacy of accomplishments. My many career transfers taught me when it is time to move on, do so with grace. You are no better, or more valued, than anyone who came before you or will come after you. Give your successors the space to do things their way.

A fundamental part of everyone's 'Success Formula' is to know yourself. There are many ways that a person does this. One of the very definitive and informative ways available to almost everyone is to take a personality assessment. The most widely used assessment these days is the Gallup – StrengthsFinder assessment. A person buys the bestselling book — *StrengthsFinder 2.0* by Tom Rath. The book allows you to take the assessment online and your results are immediate. The assessment divides the human personality into 34 traits and then ranks you in each, from one to 34. Initially you are told your top five strengths, which are the five traits at which you are strongest. The premise is to focus on your strengths as you are more likely to succeed using them than by trying to fix your weaknesses. My top five strengths in order are: 1. Maximizer, 2. Responsibility, 3. Relator, 4. Strategic, 5. Achiever. Here is an example of how each of these affected my performance.

My top strength is Maximizer. I flourish in the group dynamic. For me it is about building a team to do great things by leveraging each member's strengths. I have never been held back by what I could not do. Instead, I looked to partner with people whose skills I respected and appreciated because they were not the same as mine. I really do not care what I cannot do, but I am motivated by what I can do, with help. When I meet someone new or start working with someone for the first time, I go through an interview process without even realizing it. I want to know about their friend circle, what motivates them, what their involvements are. I am very attracted to people who own their strengths. It is easy for me to spot other people's gifts and bring them onto the team. I speak up and take charge, but I make sure everyone has a seat at the table. Team successes are so much more exciting than individual wins. Being a maximizer helped me most in my role as mayor; city government is a team. We are constantly striving to build the best community, not just a good one.

My second strength is Responsibility. I was born responsible as the oldest child. Growing up I constantly worried about disappointing my parents. Even today I seek out friends who are responsible. Responsibility is doing what you say you are going to do and taking ownership. I value honesty and loyalty in others as much as I expect it in myself. Both my career in hospitality and in our family publishing business depend on deadlines; for me deadlines are a measure of my dependability and commitment to getting the job done and taking responsibility. I am trustworthy, conscientious and a promise keeper. Being seen as responsible is a measure for me of my success.

My third strength is Relator. Relationships help me achieve success. They are a valued part of how I see any obstacle or opportunity. With friendships you can accomplish anything. I am drawn to hardworking friends. Since I worked in our town with my father, many of my friends met and got to know him over the last 20 years. I could always tell the ones he really liked; they were the ones who are still my close friends today. My dad has radar for genuine people. One friend of mine used to stop by the office from time to time to chat and catch up on local politics. I remember when my dad first met her, he would stick his head in my office just to say hello and make small talk. I could tell he was doing his 'interview' just as I do today. After a few months, you would hear his voice chuckling as he came by my office to say hi to her, "Hey, will someone give this gal a job here; she works more hours than Laura." She is a lifelong friend with whom I have worked on teams a dozen times. I had been drawn to her kindness, integrity, and work ethic. She was the backbone of every team. I love working hard with people I like and respect. A relationship only has value if I believe it is genuine. Privately I consider myself a sociable loner. I am drawn to the project-driven group dynamic because it is intense for a short period of time. My energy and enthusiasm must be constantly stoked like a fire. I am not as effective on long-term projects that revolve around meeting after meeting. I want to be always doing and reporting my progress back to the team. Since I go into every project convinced that we will be successful before we even start, I go in at 100% and when I am done, I have zero left. I am happy between projects because it is my alone time when I can spend time with my small circle of close friends. I love the balance they allow me. I have always gravitated to my teachers, bosses, and mentors because of the value I see in their time and counsel. During the down times, it is important to refill your tank.

My fourth strength surprised me because I thought it would be my number one — Strategic. I walk into every room with a plan. I was giving a speech recently to a group of business leaders and I challenged them to walk into every event, meeting, or gathering, looking for someone to compliment. Complimenting is connecting. It has nothing to do with being fake and everything to do with being open to connecting. When you walk into a room looking for opportunities to connect, you give off confident energy. I cannot do puzzles, but I can easily spot patterns in people and groups. To accomplish big things the group must be carefully put together. Too many like-minded people will not challenge anyone to be better. First, everyone at the table must want the same goal and must understand why their skill set is needed to accomplish that goal. They must hear it, not assume it. Strategic leaders provide a well thought out plan of action that can only end in success. They look for the fastest, most efficient way to get the goal results because the group will rally behind accomplishment. Part of being strategic for me is the ability to look ahead and consider the unintended consequences. Decisions are not made in a vacuum; that is why I have always valued best practices. You are rarely the first to think of something, so always take advantage of what has and has not worked for others. Use your connections to test your ideas. Work around obstacles to take the path of least resistance but move forward with resolve and determination.

My fifth strength is Achiever. Hard work pays off; it has been ingrained in me since childhood and provided a constant payoff throughout my life. My personality thrives on being busy and productive, otherwise I feel lazy. I know that sounds silly, but I have always measured myself by what I have accomplished. I was interviewed by a local magazine when I was first elected mayor. They asked me why I have been so involved in my community over the years; I replied that I did not want my kids to remember me sitting on the sofa watching TV. I wanted them to see me as someone who made a difference. Wow, how critical I was of myself. Being driven and ambitious does not mean you do not deserve time off, but I find myself defining the success of each day by what I accomplish and that leaves no time for just doing nothing. Maybe all I accomplish is cleaning the bathroom or mopping the kitchen floor (yes, I clean my own house) but when I lay down to go to sleep every night, I go into autopilot doing an inventory of the day's accomplishments. It makes me content, so I do not sweat it. Maybe that is my way of giving myself grace.

WHEN YOU LOSE

You cannot ever be totally objective in analyzing yourself. Age, intelligence, and experience do not matter. The downside of challenging yourself to achieve means you will be taking many risks. Whether these risks are well reasoned or not, you will not win them all. Be ready to ask for help from your trusted mentors, colleagues, and friends. If you live your life aiming up, there will be times when you trip, tumble, and fall. There are not any rules for how you must handle loses but pausing and reevaluating is vital to the process of moving on. I have been passed over for promotion, lost an election and ended my first marriage. Those are my biggest losses, the ones that hurt the most. Some losses get 24 hours, some are a gut punch, some make you want to hide under the covers, and some you see coming for miles.

My dad and I have watched the telephone directory business slowly fade over the last decade and a half due to technology. The yellow pages industry had an incredible run. The first yellow pages directory was published in 1883; almost 140 years ago. For our family, it paid the bills for 65 years; the last 35 years our family name was on every cover we published. For me it changed everything. I watched my dad make tough decisions, take risks, negotiate important deals. Win or lose, he always did it with class. He planned and saved for the future; even during the best times he saved every penny he could. He taught me to be realistic and to plan based on reality, not fantasy. "The numbers don't lie." Not every business works or lasts. While phonebooks have all but disappeared in urban and suburban markets, they are still widely used in rural areas and, thanks to my dad, that has bought us a few more years. Being honest about the future of our industry allowed us the time to diversify and put in place Plan B. Yes, at some point our directories will be obsolete and Dad and I will both see it as a loss, but we did not sit idly by acting like it was not going to happen.

If you live aiming up, how do you limit unforced errors? My dad taught me not to be afraid of reasonable risk. Live life preparing for opportunities, constantly studying and learning from others. All risks are not equal. Financial risks, risks that can damage or cost you an important friendship or professional relationship cannot be judged on the same scale as a personal embarrassment. Losses are necessary but not equal. I use my Strengthsfinder results to help me consider my risk tolerance. As a maximizer I am motivated by what I can achieve. I put so much into the effort that it becomes all consuming. When I come up short, it is as much about the finality of the effort as it is the ding to my ego. There is a time and place for your ego; do not let your ego manage your reasoned decision-making process. Most, if not all, driven people struggle with their ego; I certainly do. We are constantly challenging ourselves to do more and reach higher because we know we can do a great job, if just given the chance. When I was that midnight shift manager in Cincinnati, I was already planning for the day that I would run my own hotel; because I 'knew' I could do a better job than the man who never bothered to meet me. Not well reasoned thinking — my ego talking. We often define ourselves by the fancy titles on our resume. A title is only a placeholder; superpowers do not come with it, neither does automatic respect. Your effort, performance and accomplishments define you, not your title.

Do not make the mistake of worrying about your next opportunity before you have successfully (and enthusiastically) finished the job at hand. Climbers are easy to spot and rarely accomplish big things; they do not have time. All their energy is invested in strategizing over their next move. I served with an elected official years ago who had an incredible resume. They should have been the city's volunteer of the year; their name was on every board and organization in town. But as it turned out, they were a gatherer, not a doer. They served as an elected official the same way they volunteered — one foot in the door, one foot out and on to bigger things. I worked with them for years but never knew much about them. They did not have time for chit chat or pleasantries and always seemed bored with the task at hand. They were consumed with "What's next?" It takes dedication to build a trusted group of friends and colleagues that will stick with you. It takes time, effort, and grace. You build it along your own journey by being present and invested in the task at hand.

Never underestimate the long-term value of the relationships you form along the way. Someday when you need help or advice, they will be there for you. For years I marveled at an elected official who always greeted everyone with a big smile and warm handshake. I soon realized you only had their attention for ten seconds. (Actually, barely ten seconds, I timed them.) Then, like clockwork, their eyes started to wander over your shoulder. They were always on the lookout for someone better connected with whom to talk. The same happens with exhausting friends. They always travel in a posse because alone they feel insignificant. Their ego dictates they are the self-appointed leader of the gang. They never take risks, but they relish in being a roadblock to others who do. Meaningful connections are not important to either of these types. Their ego is their driving force. Do not be fooled; they are both always looking over your shoulder.

Sometimes, no matter how hard you fight and prepare, you will lose. Do not go down the failure rabbit hole. You win or lose; not win or fail. Fail is a tough word: breakdown, defeat, decline, collapse. Now those are some very depressing synonyms for failure. No wonder we are so scared to fail that we often understandably are afraid to take risks. The synonyms for risk are not any better: danger, hazard, peril, pitfall. The most qualified person does not always win, the best idea is not always selected, the person who works the hardest does not always reap the rewards. Not every great idea is embraced. I have said it before, if I cannot fix something in the middle of the night, then I will not let it keep me up. I feel the same way about losing. I will not spend time thinking about all the what-ifs. When one door closes, another door opens: ALWAYS. I will grant myself the grace to take the time I need to feel better, but I refuse to not recover.

I recently read Megyn Kelly's book, *Settle for More*. It was part of my search for a magic bullet to help me get over a frustrating political loss, small in the scheme of things but a loss none the less. I have been an avid listener of her podcast for the last year. I followed her very public yearlong feud with then Presidential candidate Donald Trump.

Despite all she has 'publicly' been through, she exudes confidence, wisdom, and humility; I needed some of that. I loved her statement about loss on page 319.

> You can use the difficult times to shore yourself up, to prove to yourself you can handle anything, or you can lament your bad luck and cry in your soup about life being unfair. One is productive, the other most certainly, is not. Tough times can be stressful, but they also have a way of centering us of shining a light through the darkness.

Yes, her book helped me. It put a few important things in perspective, things I had forgotten while I was licking my wounds. Be a mentor who shares mistakes, losses, and disappointments; be honest with your embarrassment. Leadership is quite naturally about taking risks, trying new things, and accepting that not every effort will end in success. That is why it is so important to give it your all and surround yourself with people that will lift you up. Be proud of your accomplishments and hold fast to what you value. Go into every new effort totally committed. Surround yourself with the smartest people and seek counsel from your mentors. Then let yourself breathe, knowing you have done your best. Do not let losses be defining moments but let them be gentle reminders. Give yourself permission to choose which way to go at the fork in the road. I have always loved Robert Frost's poem, "The Road Not Taken:"

> Two roads diverged in a yellow wood,
> And sorry I could not travel both . . .
> I took the one less traveled by,
> And that has made all the difference.

Sometimes losses happen because you are reaching up at the wrong time. You may have people or circumstances going against you that you cannot control. Women like to wait until the timing is perfect but that often means waiting until time runs out, or even worse, some man jumps in front of you. Go for it. Regret for not trying is much worse than always wondering — what-if. Put yourself out there, be smart but be willing to risk losing. The best leaders are humble and the fastest way to learn humility is to lose. Humiliation, embarrassment, working hard and falling short are all scary, uncomfortable feelings, but they are building blocks for being a successful leader.

You do not get a leadership trophy for participation. We have done a huge disservice to young children by valuing participation over winning and losing. Learning to lose on the little things helps you to handle losing when it is something important to you. Parents should not make excuses, raise children who are quick to blame others and cry foul when they do not get their way. Even worse, when those children do win, they have no idea how to show empathy for the loser. Our world is in dire need of empathetic leaders. It is up to us to raise them. We need leaders at every level that know how to lose with class and win with grace.

Leaders keep moving forward by taking advantage of all the resources available. Read books, listen to podcasts, watch TED talks, challenge and motivate yourself with knowledge. It becomes easier to handle the inevitable losses the stronger, smarter, and more confident you are. I could write a whole chapter (or two) on my own losses. I see value in learning from other people who have been there. One day when I was feeling sorry for myself, I searched the podcast world for inspiration. Nothing better than vacuuming while encouraging voices float through your AirPods. (Real life still goes on!) I could not believe how many choices I had — businesses, artists, writers, athletes, politicians. It felt good to know I was not alone. There is a great deal of losing going on out there! Now you might think how depressing, but most of the stories celebrated the power of the human spirit. I listened to a podcast about an author who was trying to write his second book. His first book had received huge acclaim, so much that he could not wait to start his second book, positive it would be another win. Instead, he ran into a wall. He was paralyzed by other people's expectations, and he was desperate to feel the adrenaline rush of a second success. He had decided that he had lost before he began. As someone writing my first book, all I could think was — I should be so lucky! Here I am in admiration of him because he had succeeded in his first try! What he saw as losing, I saw as winning. He had already forgotten about how much he had accomplished and was judging himself solely by what he had yet to do. Losses do not take anything away from who you are at your core and all you have previously accomplished.

When you decide on your 'next' challenge, make sure you give it your all. Be a sponge. Seek out the most knowledgeable people. Do your homework, ask questions, and listen to the answers, show everyone around you that you are willing to put in the work. Win or lose, people are going to remember how hard you worked. You never know who is watching. People may see you trip but they will also see the effort you gave and the way that you handled yourself. Someday you may be exactly the kind of fighter they want in their corner. When you least expect it, the phone will ring. When one door closes, another door opens. If you are mentoring a friend or colleague who is contemplating taking a risk, challenge them. Do not immediately get caught up in their excitement, be a supportive but reasoned resource for them. Women tend to let emotion guide decision making. As a female mentor, help them keep their decision-making fact- not fantasy-based.

1. Do your research.

2. Make your decision based on fact not fantasy.

3. Seek out trusted friends and colleagues who will challenge your enthusiasm.

4. Invest 100% of your time and effort.

5. Build a team as committed to your success as you are.

Losing is always a risk and some losses really hurt. They can be embarrassing, humbling and even make you doubt your self-worth. But you cannot lead by watching from the stands. I have a dear friend who often quotes parts of President Theodore Roosevelt's *Man in the Arena*, a part of a speech given at the Sorbonne, Paris, April 23, 1910:

> It is not the critic who counts: not the man who points out how the strong man stumbles or where the doer of deeds could have done them better. The credit belongs to the man who is actually in the arena . . . who spends himself in a worthy cause; who, at the best, knows, in the end, the triumph of high achievement, and who, at the worst, if he fails, at least fails while daring greatly, so that his place shall never be with those cold and timid souls who knew neither victory nor defeat.

Aiming up, allowing yourself to take a well-reasoned risk does not mean it will work out. High achievers, especially women, have a hard time accepting that putting in the work does not guarantee success. Sometimes the only choice you can make is an irrational choice, one where all the factors are not known or not subject to "cause and effect." I have always overprepared; maybe it is a sense of obligation. High achievers develop a success formula which usually includes hard work, proven skills and knowledge. They have such a high degree of confidence in this success formula that it biases their decision making in emotional matters. Running for political office is almost always an irrational endeavor. Increasing the number of positive factors can help the outcome but there may be negative factors in a race that no one ever knows about prior to the outcome. I offered my service, and this does not affect who I am or how good a leader I am in my real life. I learned that governing is very different than being a candidate, time for a new dream.

That was a good lesson, one that transcends politics and really speaks to leadership. When I was Mayor, I had the opportunity to travel to Cooperstown Dreams Park in New York and meet Coach Lou Presutti, the founder. Lou passed away in 2016 but he was an inspiration to the thousands of 12-year-olds who experienced the magic of playing baseball in Cooperstown Dreams Park. He spoke wisely about changing course, learning to dream a new dream. We all have dreams; some we aspire to for a very long time, but not all dreams are meant to come true. The time may come when you realize that you are not going to end up where you always dreamed you would — talent, smarts, timing. Whatever the dream, whatever the reason, it will not happen. Recognize when it is time to dream a new dream.

Do not let your ego get in the way of pivoting in a different direction. It is not the loss of a dream; it is a chance to succeed at a new one.

HERE I AM

W riting has challenged me to look back, relive some sad times and celebrate wonderful times but most importantly, remember the things that made me who I am today. Each of us takes a journey; the only thing we can be assured of is that the path will have plenty of bumps. The people I met along the way were instrumental in making me who I am today. And the journey continues. It is so important to know what you place value in and never stop investing in yourself. Leadership is not male or female. Hard work, creativity, strategic thinking, risk taking, and decisive decision making are desirable human qualities and NOT just male leadership traits. Too often when we think of these traits; we think of powerful men in positions of great responsibility. As more women step into pivotal roles, they are challenging the male leadership model. Men and women are different in how they function in their personal and professional arenas. Women make a mistake when they try to lead like men rather than embracing their uniqueness as women. We must be authentic and true to ourselves to truly shine.

Women are such important role models and, regardless of age, have so much to give. I have a mentor relationship with a professional woman that is a great example of how women who have been successful can continue to grow and improve their skill set. She is a calm decision maker; I operate in a constant state of immediacy. Listening to her methodically work through issues has taught me to be more effective by taking a few minutes to breathe before I make a decision. We can count on each other, and our relationship works effectively for both of us because:

1. We bring different perspectives to each situation.

2. There is no drama.

3. We respect each other professionally and personally.

4. We both want to learn.

5. We both want each other to be successful.

What drew me to her was her commitment to hard work and decisive decision making. We valued the same things. Sometimes we talk once a week, sometimes once a month. Seek out people who challenge your skill set and will help you fine tune your style. Look for role models in unusual places. If you are attending an event and connect with the speaker, introduce yourself and get their contact information. Are there other ways you can follow their work? You may connect with the message from someone you will never have the chance to meet. Track down their books, articles, podcasts, speeches, and interviews. Several years ago, I travelled to Washington DC for a women-in-government summit. I had the amazing opportunity to meet then Secretary of State Condoleezza Rice at her office at the State Department. A small group of us had the opportunity to visit with her and listen to her speak about her role and responsibilities. I was in awe and came away from the meeting totally inspired. When I think of her to this day, I think of poise, class, and strength. I continue to be inspired through her books, interviews, and speeches. "You get to know yourself by being outside of what you are comfortable doing," stated Condoleezza Rice.

Mentorship is about leveraging strengths. Strengths should transcend gender but too often women make the mistake of using females to commiserate with rather than learning from them. Women speak to other women differently; more emotionally. "I am so upset and need your help; I'm overwhelmed with this problem," rather than, "I'm working through an issue; I'd like to get your perspective." The well-rounded leader can do amazing things and be part of meaningful change. Having both male and female mentors is so important to a 360-degree view. I learned much about leadership from two younger male colleagues who I met through public service. Professionally we worked in different fields and were at different stages of our careers. Our mentor relationship started out with me (older and wiser) sharing knowledge and offering advice when they stepped up to run for elected office. Soon our mentor relationship transitioned to a partnership because of our commitment to good governance and willingness to take on tough issues. They shared my love of effective communication with our citizens. While I was attending events, they were utilizing video. It was an amazing tag team that benefitted the community. When Covid hit, our relationship turned to discussions about our businesses and our grave concerns for the survival of our companies as we navigated new regulations, mandates, financial worry, the health of our employees and the new, uncertain world businesses had to face. I realized that the strengths I valued in them were the strengths I could rely on to help navigate pressing issues. Both men are honest, caring, hardworking and committed in their public service. No surprise that they were the same in their businesses. Mentoring often becomes friendship as you invest in other people's successes, and they invest in yours.

Men and women are different in how they function in their personal and professional arenas. I think that is not only a good thing but something more women should embrace. Women are so great at connecting. Isn't that what leadership is about, connecting in a way that motivates others to do their best? One of the biggest challenges I see today for women is getting them to connect with others outside their immediate friend or work group. Women prefer the comfort of a reliable female friend group; it is safe and predictable. It takes me back to my days in high school. We love our cliques. We need to force ourselves into new spaces with new people. Mentoring is a give and take of ideas and experiences, often from those who see things differently than we do. It is vital to learn from other women. We miss out on so many opportunities to succeed because we are not connecting in our professional and public service. No woman should miss out on the wealth of knowledge and experience other women can share. When you mentor, you connect through shared knowledge, successes, and disappointments. I feel an obligation to contribute to the success of young women who will be leaders for the future.

Each woman leader should be authentic and true to herself. Yes, I wish I was soft spoken and sweet, but I am not. I am tough, intense, and very opinionated. I own it now but for years I hated it. Great women leaders own their style and capitalize on it. First and foremost, you must be honest with yourself. The things you care about should get the best from you. Saying yes to everything is saying yes to mediocrity. Success depends on the uniqueness we each bring to every endeavor. There is too much pressure on women to be like men because women have watched for years as the road to success is jammed with men. Many women think that is the easiest way forward, so they give away some of their uniqueness and make the significant mistake of trying to be like men in their professional lives. Surround yourself with quality friends and colleagues who are happy for your successes and supportive of you when you have failures, and I challenge you to be a woman who actively looks for an opportunity to compliment another woman. Be a team builder, not a one-woman show. Build professional relationships with women in different industries, women who can challenge you, be a mentor and find a mentor. Use your own voice. Whether you are speaking, writing a letter or email, in a casual conversation or posting on social media, be thoughtful and classy. Do not give your power away by confusing how you feel with what you want to achieve.

How you speak and how you dress sends a message. You need to ask yourself if you reflect the respect you want people to have for you. If you want to lead, then you need to be conscious of the decisions you are making when you walk in your closet every day. Yes, we live in a day and age where women are empowered to express themselves, but does it get you what you ultimately want? I believe women make a huge mistake dressing provocatively in the workplace. It is so easy to dress with style and to look fabulous, just look at Pinterest. You do not have to give up self-expression, but you do need to consider the impression you make every day on the men and women you want to lead. People are judging you all the time and they are judging you by what you choose to show them.

Leadership is really connecting in a way that motivates others to do their best. It is built on trust, loyalty, and respect. It breeds success. Reflect it in how you dress, how you speak, and what you share on social media. Be constantly aware of the people you encounter and look for opportunities to be a mentor and to be mentored. Women are so naturally gifted in making connections. We must step up and out of our comfort zone. In public service, philanthropy, and business, we bring empathy and a way of communicating that is authentic and full of purpose. What holds us back is ourselves — fear, lack of confidence, a desire not to be judged, never throwing caution to the wind. So, what if I fail this time?

Times have changed and now more than ever we need women leaders at all levels, and we must be there to lift women who are willing to step up publicly. Our entire country faced a wake-up call in 2020. When schools closed and our children started learning at the kitchen table, moms all over the country stood back and started to question their children's curriculum. For decades, as both parents joined the work force, schools took over more and more responsibility and 'teaching our kids' became much more than reading, writing, arithmetic, science, and arts. Had we unknowingly handed over too much? Now moms were attending every school board meeting; they were asking questions and demanding answers. The pandemic awakened the only thing more powerful than a sleeping giant — mothers.

God gave me two important gifts: leadership ability and a driven temperament. I also learned that with these talents comes a responsibility, even an obligation, to use them for some greater good. My calling will continue to be about giving back to my community and mentoring the next generation of women leaders. As a child I dreamed of being accepted, being part of the community. As an adult I realize it is up to me. Start with finding what moves your heart. Give your time and your treasure to the things that make you feel good and inspire you to do more. It is that great feeling we get that tells us that we are in the right place at the right time doing the right thing. I have come to realize that when you are giving to something you care about, you are giving to yourself. Take a moment to privately acknowledge it. Feel good about your contributions and do not be afraid to pat yourself on the back. Take responsibility for building up your own self confidence so that you can continue to be an agent of change. Surround yourself with people who want to see you succeed but will hold you up when you fail. Learn from those that went before you; respect the past.

My father has been the single most influential person in my life. I grew up watching him work hard and sacrifice to achieve the American Dream. When I consider the gifts I have been given and the sacrifices made for me, I feel a great sense of responsibility to both my parents. As I consider what my 'next' is, I do so knowing that the lessons taught to me by my dad will guide me. His five rules for success will be the ones I always follow as I continue to look for ways to serve my community.

1. Always keep your word.

2. Benefit from associating with successful people.

3. Do not be afraid of reasonable risk.

4. Every single day fix one thing.

5. Respect money.

It seems like I have amassed a lifetime of lessons, but I am smart enough to know there is much more to learn and much more to do. I have always known that I wanted to do bigger things, to leave my mark; I just had to believe in myself. I have gained confidence and wisdom through the years with the guidance of my father and the many mentors I have welcomed into my life. The biggest roadblocks were the ones I placed in my path. Now I look back on 32 years in the workforce and almost 14 years in elected office, dozens of boards, commissions, and volunteer organizations. I have used the gifts God gave me to make a difference in my community, in the hotels in which I worked, in our family business and with those whom I have mentored.

As I have written this book and taken you on my journey, I hope I have influenced you to look back, find your strengths, and reflect on the lessons learned along your own journey. Allow yourself to change course, walk through new doors, re-evaluate priorities and make tough decisions that may hurt. Do you have mentors in your life and are you a mentor? Have you challenged yourself to reach outside your own comfort zone? Do you surround yourself with people that lift you up and bring value to your life?

Women do have to work harder; not acknowledging that is fooling yourself and potentially setting yourself up for many disappointments. Yes, it is unfair but learning to work strategically and building a core group of supporters will pay off long term. Life is a long-term play. There are no shortcuts and little time for self-pity. Always be building for the future, never settle; if you are too comfortable, you are not in the game.

It is 6am; I am sitting at the kitchen table with a fresh cup of coffee, laptop open. My mind begins to wander. It has been doing that more and more because I know I am close to the end of writing this book. Already I am starting to worry about what I will do when this book is finished. Will there be something big to take on after this? I left elected office because I was term limited, not by choice. Writing this book helped me feel like I was still relevant. It kept me motivated after losing a big slice of my identity. I reached out to a trusted team to help me and took on writing like every other project in my career. The desire to achieve great things always pushes me forward.

EPILOGUE

When I began writing this book less than a year ago, I had no plans to run for public office again. I was looking forward to speaking engagements, luncheons and spending long weekends in New Orleans.

The human need or emotion to exercise power is one of the strongest and most basic we possess. If a person has exercised power, whether in business or public service, and been successful, it is difficult to walk away. This is not a bad thing since most people are motivated by doing good. There are political seasons, and none springs greener and more tempting than when redistricting provides a new opportunity, one you had never considered before. At least that was the intention in the beginning. Therefore, just like many rational leaders before me, I saw the stars align for a great political opportunity. As the six-month political season unrolled, events and handicaps beyond my imagination became reality and led to a political defeat. Losing is not easy for any high achiever, and we all deal with it in our own ways. I came back down to earth and immediately regained my compass on the calling that gave me great meaning before the political fever hit.

Women in leadership are faced with tremendous challenges and contradictory messages from all quarters. In this time of incredible change and disruption, women have been misled to think they should compete just like men, but this leads to very mixed and incomplete results. The absolute truth remains women are not just like men and should compete on their own unique basis. If women put all their energies into work, they deprive themselves of their need for relationships — romantic and peer. If they have not answered the question about family, then the clock is a cruel burden. Women that try to have it "all" usually pay a price in physical and emotional health.

I especially want to encourage women to do it their way — smarter and better. What this exactly looks like, I do not know. I do know I will be talking and listening to women and hope my book helps them in this quest!